T0209445

"If you want to take a serious look at yourself and come away laughing, spend some time with *Living Wisely: Open Your Life and Pour in Proverbs.* Matthew Nance has compiled a classic tonic for the soul that should be read by all of us."

- Roy J. Fish
Retired Professor of Evangelism, Southwestern Seminary

"I really enjoyed reading *Living Wisely.* Matthew offers practical applications for wisdom in everyday life. Now I am excited about re-reading it and sharing it with friends."

- Miss Harah Chon
26 year old MBA Student, Hong Kong

"Matthew has skillfully and practically integrated the timeless principles of Proverbs into daily living for us all. His candid discussion of the topics, personal openness, and varied international experiences combine to make *Living Wisely: Open Your Life and Pour in Proverbs* more than a devotional book. It is a practical manual for living as God would have us all live no matter where we live."

- C. Gene Wilkes, Ph.D.
Author of *Jesus on Leadership*

LIVING WISELY

OPEN YOUR LIFE AND POUR IN PROVERBS

— FOREWORD BY AVERY WILLIS —

LIVING WISELY

OPEN YOUR LIFE AND POUR IN PROVERBS

J. MATTHEW NANCE

WestBow Press books may be ordered through booksellers or by contacting:

WestBow Press
A Division of Thomas Nelson & Zondervan
1663 Liberty Drive
Bloomington, IN 47403
www.westbowpress.com
1 (866) 928-1240

ISBN: 978-1-9736-3649-6 (sc)
ISBN: 978-1-9736-3650-2 (e)

Library of Congress Control Number: 2018909711

Print information available on the last page.

WestBow Press rev. date: 08/24/2018

To the one I call "my precious."
Because God has given me you, *Cheryl*, as my wife,
I am most blessed among men.
And to our two fine sons,
who were the inspiration for this book.
Joshua and *Jonathan*, a major goal
of my life is accomplished
as I see you launching well into adulthood.

ACKNOWLEDGEMENT

Every human being should have parents like mine! Mother and Daddy, by your example you raised me to intuitively know how to live day by day with wisdom as my coach, and for that guidance, the mere words "thank you" fall way short. This book was shaped in a practical way by your careful reading of each chapter and in a profound way by how you raised me.

The family of believers at International Baptist Church of Hong Kong served as a sounding board for the principles on these pages. For your affirmation of these timeless truths, I am grateful. Betty Chan, you encouraged this book into reality. Nancy Mock, you carefully proofread each chapter and continued to motivate me forward. Ron Brown, you inspired me to make this book happen. Marilyn Critzer, you gave it a final once-over. Thank you all.

Heavenly Father, above all, I thank You for speaking so clearly during these two years spent probing the book of Proverbs. What You have done in my heart through this study was worth it all!

FOREWORD
by Avery Willis

Bruce Marchiano, who played the part of Jesus in *The Gospel of Matthew,* tells of a time when, shooting the movie in the middle of South Africa, he became distracted by a pretty young extra. Although he was doing everything he could to be like Jesus, he noticed her every time she walked by.

A dear Christian friend came to him one morning and said, "Good Morning, my bro! The Lord gave me a word for you this morning." He opened his Bible to the book of Proverbs and shared, "The one who winks at you plots your destruction" (Prov. 16:30).

"Does this mean anything to you?" he asked.

"Not a thing," Bruce replied.

Bruce said, "It wasn't a minute later that our new crew member drove up. She looked her usual wonderful self and smiled broadly at me, no doubt matching the smile that was beaming back at her. Then, as she passed and said good morning, she did something she'd never done before that moment. You guessed it—*she winked at me!* I couldn't believe my eyes! And as if that weren't enough, *every* time she walked by that day she winked- again and again! It gave me the scare of my life, and all attraction for that woman immediately transformed into stark terror. From that moment on, I ran the other way as fast as my sandals could take me."[1]

The power of the proverbs is proverbial!

Whenever I see a new book, I always ask the question, "Why should I read this book?" If you are like me, your busy schedule demands that there be one or more really good reasons. So, why should you read *Living Wisely?*

You will like this book because it is personal. As Matthew Nance explores Proverbs and tells his story, you may feel that he has been reading your mail or your thoughts! This book is helpful because he is willing to be vulnerable and transparent.

This is not your ordinary book. It is a fresh approach to the writings of the wisest man in history. No doubt, Solomon got his great wisdom from God. He also collected the wisest sayings from the chosen people of God. Many people value this wisdom so much that they follow a Bible reading program and read a chapter of Proverbs every day until they have read through the book twelve times a year. Matthew's fresh look at the proverbs will help you incorporate their teachings and apply them to your daily life.

Another reason to read this book is that it is written by a missionary who has experienced life in several different cultures and looks at truth from many perspectives. You will notice as soon as you begin reading that Matthew Nance is not your stereotypical missionary. He is a fun loving guy who takes a humorous approach to life. Yet, he always takes you to the truth of Scripture.

I had the privilege of going to college with Matthew's parents, and serving as a missionary with them in Indonesia. As the Senior Vice President for overseas operations of Matthew's mission board, I also watched him grow as a missionary. I have listened to his wisdom as he talked with me about some very serious matters he was dealing with on the mission field. He incorporates his fun loving approach with dead serious advice throughout the book. You will enjoy this extraordinary book.

You will find this book very practical. It comes from life experience and is easily applied to life. Matthew's application of Proverbs is both easy to make and memorable. It will make a difference in your life. Read it with joy!

Avery T. Willis, Jr
Executive Director
International Orality Network

TABLE OF CONTENTS

DANCE WITH GRANDMA!

Let The Wisdom of the Ages Teach You How to Really Move!

Do you sometimes wish you could hire a personal assistant to coach you toward a better life destination? Do you sometimes find yourself regretting what you've done or decisions you've made? Do you occasionally say "I just don't know what got into me"? Does the sweat you're putting into life seem to bring little results?

If you answered yes to any of the questions I just asked you, then surely you are interested in a recipe I found. It's a recipe for living wisely. Are you willing for life's ingredients to be remixed? Are you ready for change? Here's the recipe for wise, smart, effective living: open your life and pour in Proverbs! Hidden within these ancient Eastern sayings are life-changing secrets waiting to be discovered. As you let the wisdom coach change you, some ingredients of your life will be taken out, others added, and unexpected spices will be sprinkled in along the way. The result will be a life creatively cooked, fully baked with delicious zest oozing out, wholeness packed within, power and fragrance steaming forth, and integrity in every solid bite.

Whether you are desperately seeking a new direction or just have some vague feeling that maybe life could be better, this book is for you. Are you young enough to believe that change is possible? Are you old enough to be open to receiving guidance? I have a coach you need to meet. He is an ancient sage from the East, where I have spent twenty years of my life so far. I meet him frequently. He's way different than most westerners, but what a huge help he's been to me and to those I've introduced to him. Though he is not perfect, he teaches us from his victories as well as his mistakes. His methods are very specific, and have been tested, true and timeless. And the amazing thing is that he is available to be *your* personal assistant! More on that later. First, here's my clear challenge to you.

Begin now to build a life that works. All of the resources of heaven are at your disposal, ready to change your life. Change *is* possible. Maybe you feel that up to now life has sometimes been working against you. Let Proverbs build a life that works *for* you. Follow the way of wisdom day by day, and soon the label on your life will clearly read "Built by Wisdom."

A house is built by wisdom, and becomes strong through good sense. Proverbs 24:3

DANCE WITH GRANDMA!

I was sitting in a plane at the Bangkok airport, waiting for take-off when the announcement came. Because of a large number of transferring travelers coming from a delayed plane, we would have to wait for take-off. The people from the other plane finally began arriving by bus, boarding the plane from the rear. They came running in, and to my surprise, among them was the wife of my good friend Jaime, and their two children. I only saw them briefly from a distance as they passed me on the opposite aisle. Then came a man who looked just like my friend Jaime. He had the rounded bald head, the height, and the build of Jaime.

After take-off, I made my way up the opposite aisle to find him. Suddenly, a mischievous idea came to mind. I walked forward until I found that familiar bald head, snuck up quietly from behind, and crouched down behind his seat. Carefully and quietly, I reached up and, after quickly thumping his left ear, got back down as low as possible so he couldn't see me. I waited, but there was no response from Jaime. So I did the same to his right ear, only adding a little bit more force to the thump!

Still, there was no response. I thought, *How strange! Maybe he is asleep.* So I stood up and walked around to see his face. Though the back of the head was exactly Jaime-like, the face on the front of that head was not at all that of Jaime! I had been thumping the ears of a total stranger! How foolish I had been. How fortunate that I was still alive! I searched the plane until I positively identified Jaime's wife and kids, then told them what I had done. They laughed hysterically, and told me Jaime was not on the plane.

Leave your foolish ways behind and begin to live; learn how to be wise. Proverbs 9:6

Sometimes our assumptions need to be challenged. We think we know how to do life, but after following our own way, we see how foolish we were. What assumptions of yours hold you back from enjoying a better life? For instance, do you tend to assume that most people cannot be trusted? Or do you assume that you deserve better treatment than what is offered? Faulty assumptions lead us to wacky behavior, like thumping the wrong ear! Too often we find ourselves in tough spots of our own making. We have thumped the ear of the wrong person. At such times we may feel that life is over. The truth is that during such teachable moments life can begin to change for the better. We become more open to change.

When we've made a mess of things, it's then that we finally realize we *need* to change. Proverbs not only challenges us to change, it also shows us how change really is possible. The ancient wisdom of Proverbs gives us the practical steps of how to change.

Though you only have one life, every day is an opportunity to change the course of your life. It's never too late to change. Live each moment as a teachable moment. Don't worry so much about the times you thumped the wrong person on the ear! Begin now to build a life that works. The ancient words of Solomon, the Eastern sage, are not lofty philosophical ideals. Solomon gives us earthy, common sense insight for living life as it was intended to be lived.

So get a life! Get the truth of Proverbs working on your mental assumptions. Let Proverbs challenge your areas of faulty thinking and the negative emotions that may be holding you back. Proverbs will show you ways you didn't even know you needed to change. The big question is this: are you willing to change? There is one simple key that unlocks Solomon's treasure chest of wisdom. Here is that simple key: have a teachable attitude. Are you teachable? Take this test.

- When making decisions, do I actively seek out the opinions of others?
- Am I willing to admit my mistakes to others?
- Do I open-mindedly consider viewpoints other than my own?
- Am I willing for my life's destination to change?

Become eager to gain practical advice from others, and see how your life's destination changes.

Get all the advice and instruction you can, and be wise the rest of your life. Proverbs 19:20

My wife, Cheryl, spoils me with home cooking every day. A few years ago, our work took me to Taipei, Taiwan, for several weeks by myself. While there, I barely survived on my own cooking. Toward the end of my time there, I was running out of groceries. The frugal side of me would not allow groceries to be bought. The inner voice said "Put together whatever ingredients you have leftover, and do some creative cooking." So into the skillet went four eggs, some mushrooms, and, at the last minute, a bag of multi-colored peanut M&Ms. The resulting psychedelic omelet was delicious enough and colorful enough to patent! Ask me later about the chicken I once boiled in orange Fanta. It needs a patent, too.

Are you and I willing to let wisdom do some creative cooking with the ingredients of our lives? Follow this recipe for living wisely: open your life and pour in Proverbs. You will find yourself becoming truly intelligent.

Intelligent people are always open to new ideas. In fact, they look for them. Proverbs 18:15

In 2002, Cheryl, our two boys, and I packed up twelve years of life in Korea, prepared two bags each and moved to a creative access country. On the way from the airport to downtown in our new city, we saw local restaurants where dying animals were hanging upside down by the front door. Needless to say, we didn't have much of an appetite that day. By the next day we were hungry, but we were not yet brave enough to go out to eat. We wanted to go buy groceries, but on the way from the airport we had been traumatized by glimpses of the open market. Chickens were running around everywhere on a dirt floor where raw meat and vegetables were piled high.

I just wasn't ready to go to the market. So being a smart father, I sent our two boys Joshua and Jonathan! They were sixteen and twelve years old at the time. I told them, "Please go buy some eggs. Remember, we saw chickens running around at the market, so surely they have eggs." So, as boys do, off they went on their big adventure. When they got to the market, they felt like they had dropped in from another planet. Everyone began staring at those two big, tall white boys.

Joshua and Jonathan looked in vain for the eggs. The grandmas selling live chickens were trying to figure out what those guys wanted. To communicate, those two smart young men began giving a visual display. Twelve years of cross-cultural living had taught them many survival skills. Joshua and Jonathan began acting like chickens. They flapped their wings, squatted up and down, and squawked like chickens. "Bak bak bak BAAAK!" Not getting the results they wanted, a further step was added. When they squatted down, they pretended to lay eggs, grabbed the dropping eggs with their hands as they "laid" them, and proudly "showed" the eggs to the grandmas! Calling all their friends over to watch these two crazy foreigners, all the Grandmas started doing the chicken dance!

Then, the boys came home. "Did you get some eggs?"

"No, but we danced with Grandma!"

Through living each moment as an opportunity to learn and change, within a few months Joshua and Jonathan were ordering meals at restaurants, chatting with the locals in their language, and navigating around the city as if they had lived there all their lives. And it was all because they danced with Grandma. Life was teaching them the skills they needed not only to survive, but to thrive and enjoy. That is the way of practical wisdom. Being teachable quickly changes us into competent achievers.

When it comes to practical life skills, do you want to move from novice to expert? Here's how: dance with Grandma. She will give you wisdom. Let the wisdom of the ages teach you how to really move. When life doesn't hand you the egg you are hoping for, be creative! Try something different. Don't just have a pity party. Do a little dance. Even if you go home without an egg in your hand, you'll have a great story to tell. You'll go home wiser, and more experienced. Want to be more intelligent? Be open to new ideas and new habits. Look for those chances to dance with Grandma.

There are many benefits to opening your life and pouring in the wisdom of Proverbs.

- Wisdom will "make the simple minded clever" (Proverbs 1:4).
- Wisdom says "Let me give you common sense" (Proverbs 8:5).
- Those who find wisdom have an intuitive discretion that can mean the difference between death and life. "Discretion is a life-giving fountain to those who possess it" (Proverbs 16:22).
- The one who sets wisdom as high priority "stays on the right path" (Proverbs 15:21).
- Wisdom will give you "good planning and insight" (Proverbs 3:21).
- Wisdom says "insight and strength are mine" (Proverbs 8:4).
- A person who is wise has wholeness or integrity, and "The Lord...delights in those who have integrity" (Proverbs 11:20).
- Wisdom makes us learn things with ease. "Knowledge comes easily to those with understanding" (Proverbs 14:6). Not only is learning easy to the wise, learning gives an emotional lift. "The wise person makes learning a joy" (Proverbs 15:2).
- Those who are wise have insight into things of the heart. "Wisdom is enshrined in an understanding heart" (Proverbs 14:33).
- Wisdom makes a person live upright, and "the path of the upright is easy" (Proverbs 15:19).

Are you ready to become strong, intelligent, competent, and relaxed through the common sense that wisdom gives? Read on, my friend, and wisdom will begin to work on you. You will begin to work wisdom into your life. The wisdom coach will begin to work *for* you. All this work needs time, so read slowly. Like a recipe waiting to be cooked, each chapter is very full of potential. Try the recipe out, and experiment with it. Make it your own, and notice changes in your life.

Move forward through a chapter only after wisdom has become deeply rooted in your thoughts and habits. Don't think you can cruise through this book quickly and put it back on the shelf. Read one section, and then give it time to thump you on the ear. Your assumptions may need challenged. Then you need time to react and let change happen. Take a month for each chapter if you need to. Start with a specific area in which you know change is needed in your life–money management, sexual purity, or whatever. Skip to that chapter first and let wisdom work first in the area where you have the highest motivation. Then come back to the other chapters. Don't just read; re-read. And rebuild. Let wisdom build the house of your life. Put on your dancing shoes and go find Grandma.

COOL IT!

Break Free from Anger!

It was slowly brewing inside of me, darker than the blackest coffee. Just let someone jiggle my pot a little bit and my anger might come spewing out at random. Culture shock over time will do that to the best of men. Though our family was really enjoying our new life in Korea, there was a part of me that secretly grew more and more upset each time things did not go according to the mental roadmap I had brought with me from the States.

Each day, professional people pushers paid by the government pushed me into the subway Train. Once inside, bodies were packed in like sardines, and because they had all eaten fish and *kimchi* (fermented, spicey cabbage) for breakfast, they smelled as bad as sardines! I was at least a foot taller than all of them and even had to duck my head to keep from hitting the top of the train. The strong *kimchi* smell rose to the top of the train and stuck there in my angry, fire-breathing nostrils!

At my destination I found myself, along with other compressed bodies, being spewed out from the steaming, stuffy train innards! I found that my clothes had become permanently pressed with wrinkles! At least I could be thankful that I had not, as had happened on many days before, been spewed out at a stop prior to, or after, my hoped for destination!

I wobbled from the subway station to class. There I studied what they told me was one of the most difficult languages in the world to learn. I soon realized they had lied to me. Korean is not one of the most difficult languages. It is *the* most difficult! Four hours of language school every day left my head senseless, even at times to the point of forgetting where I was or why I was!

Language was one life challenge. Transportation was another. What would have taken fifteen minutes by personal car in the States took over an hour by public transportation, and brought lots of tests of character. People were talking about us right in front of our faces, and pointing at various parts of our bodies, which they found too big or too small! They laughed at our attempts to speak Korean, and even verified how masculine our little boys were by pulling their pants down to do a hand check of their equipment!

Just let me at these people, I thought, *and I'll show them how I feel about all this!* Missionaries cannot get mad, right? Missionaries wear halos! I just stuffed the anger deep down into a secret room of the heart, but there was no way to lock the door. It came out against random people. I was rude to the taxi driver who picked up other customers on my nickel.

I gave some of my anger to people who bumped me on the street or tried to sell things to me at a foreigner's price. Even the store salesman, who did nothing wrong except laugh at my strange Korean, received a portion of my rage.

When life doesn't go as we planned, we feel loss of control. We attempt to regain control by demanding our way. However, we then find that our unleashed anger has only made the other person feel threatened, causing a reaction of anger toward us. This response fuels more rage within us, and the whole scene escalates out of control.

During the first few months of life in Korea, I found my anger button being pushed much too often. Though your experiences may be different from mine, maybe life has given you some serious challenges. You expected life to be fair to you, but others took advantage of you. Maybe your anger button has been pushed one too many times.

Here's a test to determine the amount of anger inside you. Take a personal inventory. Ask yourself these questions:

- Am I secretly mad because I had high hopes in someone who is not meeting my needs?
- Is turmoil often brewing just under my surface?
- Do I often say things that are secretly designed to be cutting or cruel to others?
- Do I enjoy causing others around me to get cross with each other?
- Do I sometimes bully others in some way?
- Is there someone who I am not willing to forgive?
- Do I withdraw from people to live in my own world? Everyone gets along there!

If you answered yes to any of the questions, anger is a

bigger part of your life than it needs to be. If you had four or more yes answers, your life may be out of control with anger.

Every minute that you are angry robs you of sixty seconds of happiness! Life is too short to waste it being angry. To break free from an angry lifestyle, let's look at three ways anger is displayed and four ways to change anger habits.

THREE WAYS THAT ANGER IS EXPRESSED

1. Verbal Abuse of Others

The mouth of a good person is a deep, life-giving well, but the mouth of the wicked is a dark cave of abuse. Proverbs 10:11 (The Message)

Some of us are good at bad-mouthing others. We know just the thing to say to push someone else's anger button. Mark Twain tried to control his anger but finally gave this advice about what to do with it in the end:

"When angry count to four. If very angry, swear."
-Mark Twain

Americans live in a society that thinks it is fun to cut down others. We cut down others in an effort to get a laugh or make ourselves look better than they do, but in so doing Proverbs says our mouths have become dark wicked caves (Proverbs 10:11).

Some of us think we have the spiritual gift of criticism. Others of us are not so good at verbal abuse. We would love to be able to tear into others, but we just don't seem to be able to do so. The poor Quaker dairy farmer was such a man. He owned an ornery cow.

Every time he milked her, it was a clash of two wills. This particular morning, she was unusually irritable, but he was determined to endure the session without so much as a cross word. As the farmer began to milk her, ol' Bossy stepped on his foot with all her weight. He struggled silently, groaned a little under his breath, pulled his foot free, then sat back down on the stool. She then swished her tail in his face like a strong whip. He merely leaned away so it wouldn't be able to reach him. Next, she kicked over the bucket, which by then was half full of warm milk. He started over, mumbling a few words to himself, but he never lost his cool.

Once finished with the ordeal, he breathed a sigh of relief, picked up the bucket and stool, and as he was leaving, she hauled off and kicked him against the barn wall twelve feet away! That did it. He stood to his feet, marched in front of his cow, stared into those big eyes, and as he shook a long bony finger in her face, he shouted, "Thou dost know that I am a Quaker. Thou dost know also that I cannot strike thee back. But I can sell thee to a Presbyterian!"[2]

This is not just a mouth issue. It is a heart issue. Just because you don't say it, does not mean that you don't think it. If we want to change the way we speak, we must change the way we think. What happens if we don't change? If unkind thoughts and words become a habit, soon we will secretly and perversely *enjoy* getting other people stirred up against us and against each other.

2. Purposeful Sabotage of Relationships

A hot-tempered man stirs up dissension.
Proverbs 15:18 (NIV)

Ever notice how people with pent-up anger don't have many close friends? They have slowly alienated themselves from even the most patient and forgiving saints! And they can't stand to see other people relaxed and having fun together.

It's as if the angry person is saying, "If I can't enjoy stable, close relationships with others, then I'm going to make sure that you don't either!" He or she sets out to split apart what would have otherwise been good relationships.

A perverse man stirs up dissension, and a gossip separates close friends. Proverbs 16:28 (NIV)

Even though we know it's off limits, there is the potential in each of us to enjoy the power we feel when we meddle around in the relational territory of others. We plant a few negative seeds of thought between the people we hope to relationally sabotage. We even spiritualize our meddling by saying, "I share this with you only so that you can pray more effectively!"

Men and women may tend to display anger differently. Men may seem more prone toward showing their anger through physical violence. Women may be particularly quick to find twisted satisfaction in stirring up bad vibes between other people. Ladies, I challenge you to realize that such a tendency only shows an anger issue within yourself. Sisters, lay aside all forms of gossip. Stop causing bad relations between others. You are made of better stuff than that!

This is not just a lady issue. Men do this as well. In the business world, it is called passive aggression. Men, if you are angry with someone at work, and take it out on him by bad-mouthing him to your associates, you are clearly acting as a perverse man, stirring up dissension. What you are doing may give you the temporary satisfaction of revenge, but how will you feel if that man is demoted, or loses his job because of your slander? In the end, slandering others only hurts your own reputation.

3. **Physical Violence**

Better to meet a bear robbed of her cubs than a fool in his folly. Proverbs 17:12 (NIV)

The ancient man of wisdom uses the picture of an angry mama bear robbed of her cubs to show us how easily human anger erupts into physical abuse. If you mess with her cubs, watch out for that mean mama bear! Anger makes bears—and people—crazy.

We each have times when we act like our cubs have been stolen. To my own embarrassment, I share with you a darker page from my own history book.

We lived in Sang Ah Apartments in Tang Sang Dong of Seoul. Sang Ah is a high rise complex, where over ten thousand closest friends attempt to enjoy the same little postage stamp of land. To escape the density, I would run to the Han River and jog a loop around Yoido Island. I suppose the anger from continual cross- cultural stress started to be released in my running, as I found myself on cruise control at high speed.

Then from my left I heard two young male voices shouting at me. "Hey American, (Expletive) you!" Most Koreans are fond of Americans, but there are a few young Koreans that think all the problems on the peninsula are the result of the United States sticking its nose into the affairs of other nations. For them, a glimpse of an American is a chance to practice saying the unkind words they learned from American movies! Before you know it, my body cruised right on over to those noodle-sucking, foul-mouthed foes, and seeing the noodle bowls that were already right at the ends of their noses, I proceeded to flip those bowls rapidly upward, sending hot water and noodles all over those two poor guys! Of *course,* I did it in the name of Jesus!

Proverbs talks about a mama bear's anger when her cubs are stolen. I have my own version of that verse. Better to catch a tiger by the tail than to mess with a missionary in culture shock!

My tendency toward anger is not something of which I am proud. Foe One and Foe Two, I am sorry for how I caused you to lose face that day. The least I could have done was to stick around to wipe your faces clean, but I just kept running. I came to your country to love you into God's Kingdom, but you didn't see any love at all in my actions. My anger vented on you caused shame to you and to the One who sent me.

They had me outnumbered two to one. It's amazing that they didn't come after me to even the score. Had they been Texans, they might have pulled the shotgun out of the pickup truck, just to put some fear in me. Looking back now, we can see how it was a great blessing to have raised our boys in places that are primarily non-violent. In Korea, it is against the law to own a gun. In China, it is against the law for the Han people (92% of the population) to sell a knife that is not a cooking utensil. In Thailand, the greatest sin to avoid is displaying anger toward others.

Sure, East Asian societies have their share of violence and anger-based problems, but as a whole you will find Eastern peoples to be very kind and respectful of others. These cultures highly value making sure that other people do not lose face. Certainly, the people of Asian societies as a whole are far less prone than Americans to verbally tear down other people. They tend to be much more polite in how they treat others.

We, at times, return briefly for a few months to the United States. I am proud of America and weep on those rare occasions when I am able to stand with my feet on the soil of my homeland, go to a baseball game and hold my hand over my heart while pledging my allegiance to the land I love. On the other hand, I am embarrassed at how our supposedly Christian nation holds up heroes who solve their problems by telling people off.

Our American young people make heroes of professionals who hurt others by kicking, hitting, slapping, and terminating. We root for the guy with the fastest six-shooter. We spend hours on video games that define winning as killing the most people. We admire the tough guy who doesn't take any bull from anybody.

We have become programmed to laugh at and even to enjoy a dreadful thing called *physical violence.* We bring it daily into our homes through television and games. With so much violent garbage going into our brains, it's no wonder road rage is on the rise and prisons can't be built fast enough to house all of our society's mad men.

It's time to protect our own households from the media bombardment of violent scenes. Practice mind over media. Turn it off and enjoy an evening of relaxed conversation or interactive table games!

Physical violence is not just a problem in the scenes depicted on dramas; it's not just on our streets and in the back alleys. Unfortunately, it is also common in our homes among family members. Those we should love the most dearly have somehow become those we abuse. Now I must ask you clearly: Is abuse of any kind a secret part of the way your family operates? If you are involved in giving or receiving verbal or physical abuse, don't let it go on any longer. Admit that it is seriously diminishing the quality of your life and the lives of others. You need help from outside your family. Confide in someone who has the resources to help you get free of abusive anger.

Has your anger issue escalated to the point where you are abusing others? You're not just kicking the dog, or pointing your bony finger in the cow's face. You're taking out your frustrations on those you love. It's time to cool it. There is a remedy. God created you. He is the one you need to call on to reach inside of you and re-create you into a person who lives a lifestyle above anger.

Again, the issue is not just a physical one, it is a spiritual one. Violence is only the result of a heart that has not yielded itself completely to the healing power of Christ's love. Violence is merely the extreme version of getting your own way. The wise person's life is not about getting his way. It is about living God's way. Here's God's ancient eastern wisdom for helping us break free from anger.

FOUR HANDLES ON ANGER

Handle Number One: Learn to live at peace with imperfection.

Better a patient man than a warrior.
Proverbs 16:32 (NIV)

Anger flares up when things do not go *our* way, on *our* time-table. We have fooled ourselves into thinking the universe revolves around our every whim. We want instant gratification, and we throw a little fit if we don't get it! We believe there is great value in attacking life like a warrior, but we don't know the value of waiting patiently.

Men really are wild at heart. It's not new knowledge. Solomon was well aware of it thousands of years ago when he described men as warriors and conquerors of cities. We have the call of the wild within us. We want to conquer outer space! Explore the unknown! Attack before others have a chance to attack us! We love to wrestle. We want to conquer the world, and we expect to do it right now!

Impatience shows that we doubt God's sovereignty over our lives. We question His goodness and grab what good we can for ourselves. We fear that He will not finish what He started in us, so we huff and puff and finish it for Him. We doubt His provision and become the take-charge warrior in search of our own provisions. We see change needed in the lives of those around us, so we put on the armor of anger and become a change- agent warrior. Our anger shows how frustrated we are when we play God but do not have an omnipotent snap in our fingertips.

In our addiction to speed, we rob ourselves of the excitement of waiting to see what surprising changes God will bring into our lives in His time. If God told you how long you would have to wait to see your dream or desire fulfilled, you might lose heart. Thank God He doesn't tell you! Sometimes, He chooses to change our dreams rather than to fulfill them! He changes them into things which will bring Him glory. Want peace in an imperfect situation? Relax, and confidently depend on God.

Handle Number Two: Forgive Others.

People with good sense restrain their anger; they earn esteem by overlooking wrongs. Proverbs 19:11

What kind of man could possibly be better than a warrior? The better man is the patient, forgiving man, that's who: a man who has learned how to control the power within himself. It's not that all males have to go on ADD medication and become calm! However, we must channel our warrior energy for good. It takes more of a man to forgive than it does to commit revenge. Men, before you go off to explore outer space and conquer others, learn to conquer the inner space of your own anger. Learn to overlook the wrongs that people have done against you.

Anyone can pay back anger for anger. You can choose to forgive. It takes a superior man to forgive. When you payback meanness with kindness, you are treating others as God has treated you. You are most like God when you forgive.

Forgiveness is never easy. It always requires dying. Once

you are dead to sin, it is easier to forgive, because you realize that you have been forgiven. My problem is that I tend to think of my sins as mistakes and your sins as terrible acts against God. The truth is my sin warrants death. First it required the death of Jesus. Now it requires the death of me, my wants, and my Grudges. Once dead, I can forgive.

Right now, think of the ones who have genuinely wronged you. What do you gain by remaining angry at them? Having pent up anger at others is like your drinking poison and expecting it to kill someone else.

You cannot change what others have done, but you can ask God to change your heart. God can change how you respond to what they did to you. Would you be willing, for your own sake, to forgive them? Picture a particular person before you. Picture what he or she did to you. Now say to him, "I forgive you." Then put the event in a folder file in the computer of your mind. Highlight that file on the screen of your mind. Now click delete. Then go to your deleted items folder and click delete all. Your mind then says, "Are you sure you want to permanently erase these records?" Click "yes" and be done with anger toward that person.

Handle Number Three: Pre-determine how you will respond when anger flares.

Better a…man who controls his temper… Proverbs 16:32 (NIV)

How do you control your temper? It's not something that you can decide at the moment the anger flares. It's already too late. You must come up with a specific plan of how you will handle yourself *before* emotions get control of you. For me, it occasionally means...

- leaving the room when things get heated up, regardless of the pressure put on me to hang around
- taking a long walk to calm my short temper
- thinking through *why* I feel anger
- asking for God's wisdom for the situation
- coming up with the words to express my thoughts without attacking the person involved
- going back into the situation with a calm spirit, ready to attack the problem, not the person, until together we come up with a solution with which we both agree.

Moderation is better than muscle.
Proverbs 16:32 (The Message)

A key to winning over sudden outbursts of rage is developing a plan of action that works for you, and the moment you feel angry, put your plan into action. Do that consistently, and soon, through God's power, you will be taming the terminator within you.

Side stepping an explosive situation does not mean becoming a door mat and not telling others how you feel. It means finding a way to solve problems without blowing a gasket! It's honesty without meanness. It's all right to be irritated and express irritation, as long as you attack the problem, not the person.

Have you heard of the X, Y, Z formula for expressing your feelings without attacking someone? Here it is. "In situation X, when you do Y, I feel Z." Need a for instance? "When we are watching television together (X), and you change the channels without asking me (Y), I feel that I have not been regarded as an equal viewer (Z)!" Try using the formula to help you express, *without* hurtful words, how you feel about the action that irritates you. Make sure to state the situation, the action, and how you feel as a result.

Handle Number Four: Refuse to accept anger as a cultural norm.

Better a patient man than a warrior, a man who controls his temper than one who takes a city. Proverbs 16:32 (NIV)

Notice that when Solomon speaks of anger, he talks about men. Women certainly get mad and may do so in a way that can be more creatively cruel than something males may be able to produce. Verbal abuse and relational sabotage seem to happen equally among men and women, but physical abuse or rage seems to be primarily a male problem.

Mockers stir up a city, but wise men turn away anger.
Proverbs 29:8 (NIV)

One root of the problem may be our cultural definition of a real man. We are right to include the rough side of men in our definition of masculinity. We are warriors, conquerors, hunters, and explorers. We don't need to apologize for any of that or buy in to a culture that wants to calm us down by making us effeminate. Solomon did not say that a warrior was bad. However, he did say that there is a better kind of man. Our problem is that we often stop short before we get to the better parts of being a real man.

Society says that we must "be real; be authentic." We act as though this cultural value of masculine authenticity gives us a license to treat other people however we want. We must redefine what it means to be real. Today's culture says that we must be true to our inner self. We must let it all hang out. Our culture has placed such a high value on being authentic, that we allow anger as a cultural norm. The ancient wise man Solomon tells us out of what stuff a *real,* authentic man is made.

A *real* man is patient. A patient man is better than a warrior. A *real* man is wise. *Real* men are in the process of becoming more like *the* Real Man, Jesus Christ, through God's wisdom.

A *real* man keeps himself under control. A *real* man has the power of rushing water, which could crash beyond the borders of the river and flood civilization, but instead the water is channeled to produce electricity.

A *real* man has the energy of a wild horse but has allowed himself to be tamed so that the Master at the reins can rule life's direction and speed.

A *real* man has fire within him. He chooses not to use that fire to destroy but to burn like a campfire that provides warmth and camaraderie. A *real* man is too big to have little tantrums of rage. Men, don't let some small thing make a big guy like you angry.

There are two sides to dealing with anger. So far we have looked at dealing with your own anger. Let's close with a brief look at how to deal with the anger of others.

FIVE DON'TS WHEN DEALING WITH ANGRY PEOPLE

1. **Don't respond to anger with anger!**

Mockers stir up a city, but wise men turn away anger.
Proverbs 29:8 (NIV)

A fellow was told by his doctor that he had rabies. When he heard the news, the patient pulled out paper and pen and began writing. Thinking the man was making out his will, the doctor said, "Rabies won't kill you. There's a cure."

"I know, I know," said the man. "I'm making out a list of all the people I'm gonna bite first!"[3]

Revenge is the greatest instinct in the human race.
-Friedrich Nietzsche

Sometimes people just want to see you get mad. They rattle the cage just to hear the tiger roar. Just give them a soft answer instead. It turns away wrath. My friend, Jeff Clark of Montana, says his dad used to say, "Don't wrestle pigs. You get muddy and they enjoy it. Afterwards, you come out smelling like them!" Engaging in conflict with an angry person is just like wrestling with a pig.

2. **Don't be passive! During conflict, step up to the plate as a peacemaker.**

A hot-tempered man stirs up dissension, but a patient man calms a quarrel. Proverbs 15:18 (NIV)

Often, when two people are at each other's throats, it takes a third party to cool both sides down. Learn to be that impartial third person of peace that others can trust to bring unbiased resolution. Such a person is rare. Become someone known for calming quarrels, and you will be sought out as a peacemaker. When you hear physical violence occurring next door, go over and ask to borrow a cup of sugar! You will provide them with an accountability check. Then they'll know if they continue day after day in anger, it's going to cost them a lot of sugar!

3. **Don't try to protect a hot-tempered man from what comes his way!**

A hot-tempered man must pay the penalty; If you rescue him, you will have to do it again. Proverbs 19:19 (NIV)

I once had a tennis partner who was better than I was, but easy to beat! All I had to do was win about three humiliating shots in a row, and his anger kicked in. From that point on, his tennis was lousy! You let anger overcome you, and you are the loser!

People who fly into a rage always make a bad landing.
-Will Rogers

There are some who think the squeaky wheel should get the grease; the one who displays the most unhappiness should be the most royally pampered. These people think we should all walk around on tip toe, treading lightly around angry people. They say, "Do whatever it takes to keep the mad man happy so he won't blow his top!" I did a Greek word study on that concept and found that the New Testament has a word for it, "baloney." In the Old Testament Hebrew, the same root word is pronounced "Hog wash!"

If you pamper someone who is angry, you are allowing him to manipulate you with his mood. Don't try to protect him from the natural consequences of his anger. Don't lie to cover up what the angry person does. If he throws something and breaks the television screen, it shouldn't be replaced anytime soon! The wisdom of Solomon tells us not to passively allow abuse. Call anger into accountability.

4. Don't make friends with an angry man.

Do not make friends with a hot-tempered man, do not associate with one easily angered, or you may learn his ways and get yourself ensnared. Proverbs 22:24-25 (NIV)

The late baseball manager Billy Martin wrote a biography about himself, called *Number* 1. He writes of a hunting trip he took with Mickey Mantle. They went to a ranch that Mantle knew. When they got to the ranch, Mantle told Martin to wait inside the car while he went into the ranch house to check in. The ranch owner, as always, gave Mantle permission to hunt, but then he asked Mantle to do him a favor.

"My pet mule is going blind. I need to put him out of

his misery, but I just haven't got the heart to do it. Would you shoot him for me?" Mantle agreed.

As he was walking back to the car, he thought of a trick he could play on his friend waiting in the car. Pretending to be angry, he got in the car and slammed the door shut.

"What's wrong?"

"The old guy said we can't hunt on his land anymore! I argued with him about it, and he got angry at me! I'm so mad at him now, I'm going to drive down to his barn and shoot one of his animals!"

He floored the gas peddle and steered the car toward the barn.

"You can't do that!"

"Just watch me!"

At the barn, Mantle leaped from the car with rifle in hand, ran into the barn and shot the mule. But when he came back to the car, his friend was gone. And so was his friend's rifle. Mickey heard two loud shots behind him.

"What are you doing Martin?"

Billy's face was red with anger. "We'll show that old man! I just killed two of his cows!"

Anger is very contagious. "Anger" is one letter short of "danger." You may think you can make friends with an angry person for the purpose of changing him, but he is more interested in changing *you* into an angry person. He knows he will keep pushing different anger buttons until he finds one that gets you mad at the world, like he is. There are anger pushers who want to get you addicted to the stuff. When people like that want to become your friends, spouse, or business partner, just stay away. They will bring you down.

5. **Don't be surprised when your lifestyle of integrity causes others to react in anger!**

Bloodthirsty men hate a man of integrity and seek to kill the upright. Proverbs 29:10 (*NIV*)

For the person seeking to live with integrity in today's world, it's a jungle out there! You must be prepared to cut your way through the jungle. If you are serious about pleasing God, many people will not be pleased. They will make a game out of trying to get you to break your principles. Then, when that doesn't work, they will try to kill your spirit. When it happens, don't think it's some strange thing.

They did the same to Jesus. One of His own betrayed Him. That in itself would tick off you or me. However, Jesus was not angered. A mob of angry soldiers surrounded Jesus to take Him away, and one of them approached Him to arrest Him. Unlike many young men when being arrested today, Jesus did not respond in anger. How could He remain so calm? He knew that God had a plan in it all. It was Peter, the impulsive warrior, who swung a sword at the guy's head! Peter was still in the process of becoming, still using brute muscle strength to solve problems. In his crazed rage, he only managed to cut the guy's ear off.

What was Jesus' response to Peter, and to the soldier? Jesus showed more compassion for His enemy than He had for Peter. He rebuked Peter, but restored the guard's ear to its place. Jesus was able to control His own emotions under the greatest of stress.

Jesus was not just controlling his anger at that point. His

heart had been given fully to the Father. He had died to his own desires. He knew the Father was in control.

Anger occurs when we get frustrated because we feel loss of control over our situation. We must die to self, realizing we were never meant to be the ones in control. This is our Father's world. When we surrender to Christ's lordship over us, we acknowledge His control. Through His Spirit living within us, may you and I break free from anger.

TIRED OF PLAYING VOCATIONAL TRIVIAL PURSUIT?

Proven Methods of Failure and Success on the Job

A paycheck is a good thing. A paycheck from work that you enjoy is even better. Have you noticed how some people just go to work in order to make money, while other people seem to really enjoy their work? Some consider work as an unfortunate necessity, as just a means of making a living, but others get a great deal of satisfaction from their work. There are people who live vocationally "in the zone," while some never seem to care about their work. The difference is not in the amount of money made. The difference is in whether a person is constantly drained by their work, or more alive because of their work. Which best describes you? Does your work energize you, or are you tired of playing vocational trivial pursuit?

Mr. Im Bong Su was our security guard. We lived in a high rise apartment complex in Taejon, Korea. To leave our apartment each day, we rode the elevator down, and then walked past Mr. Im's guard shack. Not all guards put their heart into their work. We had lived in other places where the guard inside the shack was usually sound asleep! But *not* Mr. Im! As soon as he saw us coming out of the elevator, he bounded out of the guard shack, walked briskly up to us, stuck both thumbs high up in the air, and said with enthusiasm, "Have a good day!" Our sons liked him so much that they would go hang out with him inside his guard shack.

Recycling is big in Korea. Everyone must sort their trash, wash all the trash, and then put it by category in one of six bins at the bottom of the apartment building on the set day of the week. In most places we lived, the security guard would sit in his heated shack watching us stumble out of the elevator with six different kinds of trash. It seemed to bring the guard enjoyment watching us shiver and struggle to get our trash to the containers and then sort it. But not Mr. Im. on trash day, as soon as the elevator door opened, he was already there waiting to help us with our trash. He would whistle as he helped us sort our trash. Then when we finished the job together, he put two thumbs up high in the air and said with an enthusiastic smile, "Have a good day!" It's no wonder our stairwell got the city trophy for "Cleanest Trash"! Mr. Im enjoyed his work. He put his heart into it. He loved us. He even loved our trash!

Is work just about making money, or was it intended to bring fulfillment into our lives? In the Bible, work and worship are intertwined. God gave us work as a means to worship and enjoy the Creator. Work was given to man as a part of the creation package. God pronounced the entire package, work included, as "good," and even "very good." Work is not, despite popular opinion, something that God tagged on after creation as a way to punish man for his sin.[4] God designed work to energize us and give us His style of compassionate dominion over this earth.

Vocationally, God wants us to triumph. Being triumphant on the job is not always easy. Do you know what triumph is? "Triumph" is just *umph* added to try!"[5]

Maybe you once had passion about your work, but you've lost it. You've tried, but it's gone. Now, it's time to try again. Add *umph* to that try. Triumph!

God wants us to find work we can be passionate about. He wants us to be more alive because of our work. He wants us to fill this earth and subdue it. Those are the first commands God gave us. used in the way that God created them, the physical things of this earth, including "secular" work, are very good. When we do daily work in a way that honors Him, work and worship intersect. When we are genuinely passionate about our work, life has meaning. Our vocations cause us to have dominion, to triumph. God isn't necessarily more honored by our choosing a church related vocation than He is by our doing regular jobs out in the real world. Here is the note on God's message board today:

> *Needed:*
> *People out doing*
> *Everyday business*
> *as God's business*

Why work? Many people see work as one big rat race. The rats are racing to gain status symbols. Who will get to the cheese first?

There are nicer cars, beautiful clothes, and luxurious life-styles awaiting those who win the rat race. The problem with a rat-race view of work is that even if you win the race, you are still a rat.

Instead of chasing the tails of the rats in front of you, chase after the work you enjoy doing. Develop the skills God has given you. Don't try to become someone else. Become the best *you*. Become a true craftsman. Aim for excellence in your own unique area of expertise. Your work will not go unnoticed. "Do you see a man skilled in his work? He will stand before kings; he will not stand before obscure men" (Proverbs 27:18, NASV). Even if you think your skill is not all that special, put your heart into your work. Your attitude will not go unnoticed. As a security guard, Mr. Im's primary skill was not a particularly difficult one. It did not require a university degree. Nevertheless, it caused the city mayor to take notice.

Though developing skill in a vocation takes time, it takes more time for some than it does for others. The tipping point toward failure or success is not the situation we find ourselves in, but how we respond to that situation, and who we are becoming. Success in the workplace is a combination of skill development, character, and a flexible attitude that puts your heart into the work. The wisdom coach of Proverbs provides us with some insightful reasons why some people struggle to gain ground at work while other people find success in their vocational life.

WAYS SOME PEOPLE SABOTAGE THEIR OWN CAREER SUCCESS

Here are four ways that people mess things up on the job. For the sake of your own career development, check to make sure these things are not a menacing part of who you are. What is the number one reason for failure in a career?

Laziness

Like vinegar to the teeth and smoke to the eyes, so is the lazy one to those who send him. Proverbs 10:26 (NASV)

Have you ever been at a campfire, and the smoke followed you regardless of where you move? That's because smoke follows beauty! It's so irritating when smoke gets in your eyes. You stumble to a smoke-free place around on the other side of the fire, and your eyes finally stop burning. Then there comes that smoke again!

Lazy people are like that smoke. They are a constant irritation, both to those they know personally and to society in general. Lazy people are mooches. They think hard work is beneath them. They are too good to get their hands dirty. Wanting to *take* things from this world, the lazy feel they are above having to contribute to this world. Expecting their friends, co-workers, the government, and relatives to always take care of them, they seldom take care of others. They are a constant irritation. Please, for your own good, and the good of those around you, don't be a lazy mooooch!

Lazy people drain our nation's economy. Instead of going out to get work, they find out just how many ways there are to get money from the government. They are not only a costly nuisance to society; they put the future of our nation in danger, a danger actually equal to that of terrorists who seek to destroy our nation. "One who is slack in his work is brother to one who destroys" (Proverbs 18:9, NIV). Laziness will destroy a nation. The laziness of the rich can destroy the moral fiber of a nation just as quickly as the poor refusing to work can destroy the economy.

This past weekend I visited a lamp factory. I watched workers who had begun their work day at 8:30 in the morning. They took an hour break for lunch, an hour for supper, and, though it was past eight in the evening, they were still working hard. once they finally finished work, they gathered to sing praises, pray for each other, and apply the Word of God to their daily lives.

These workers make only about one hundred thirty U.S. dollars per month, but they are very happy to be making that much money. They don't spend all their income on themselves, but instead they send more than half of their income back to their extended family in the village. It doesn't seem to matter to them how much they sweat to make a product and earn a livelihood for their extended family. There's not a lazy bone in their bodies.

What about America? We are a great nation with a rich heritage of hard work. However, these days we are being seduced by ease and luxury. We have become so smart, so advanced, so computerized, so drive-through oriented, so in love with the easy life that we are not willing to do jobs that require hard work, *even if the pay is good!* We let those jobs go to foreigners and then complain about so many foreigners doing American jobs!

Lately, we have even classified nursing as a dirty job, and immigrants seem to be the primary ones who are now willing to care for people in our hospitals and nursing homes. As a nation, during our agricultural and industrial past, we worked hard. Now, in the information age, we are in danger of slipping into laziness as a life style. Watch out, America! We have met the enemy who destroys, and he is us.

The book of Proverbs tells us the lazy person is a nuisance to "those who send him." The one sending him is his employer. Bosses around the world are looking for hard workers. You may have graduated from Harvard with an MBA. Maybe you have been groomed by the best in the business for an executive position. Do you have good looks, a preppy wardrobe, and a way of winning people with your words and smile? Those are all good things that might get you hired, but are you *lazy?* That laziness thing will get you fired.

What do you do with yourself while the boss is not looking? Do you work hard only while the boss is looking? That's laziness. Successful people don't work hard for the boss's sake. They work hard because they want to contribute to the organization, because they want to develop as a person, and because it is the right thing to do. When you do the right thing, you feel good about yourself and about life.

Yes, I am aware that most jobs have some downtime where there is seemingly nothing to do. In your idle time at the workplace, *find* something to do that improves the company. Help someone else with his work. Talk with others about potential improvements. If you have spare time at work, then develop a project proposal for suggested innovations and submit it to your boss. Do so without any critical attitude. He may put you in charge of one of those needed innovations.

Have spare time on your hands at work? Go back over your work again and pay strict attention to the little details. Not being thorough with the small details is laziness. Ask someone else to double check your work for you, and in exchange, you check his work. Some people goof around and then do a rush job on the work at the last minute. That's laziness. Get your deadlines met without dilly dallying around until the day it's due.

Are you thinking of reasons why you can't do something for the company during your idle time? "The lazy person is full of excuses, saying, 'If I go outside, I might meet a lion in the street and be killed!'" (Proverbs 22:13). Are you making excuses for not working hard? Young lady, are you saying, "Well, if they don't give me any work to do, what else am I supposed to be doing? The fact that I'm sitting at my work station just chatting online with my friends is really my boss's fault." That's an excuse that shows a lack of initiative. Go tell your boss you have extra time and want more work.

Young man, when the boss tells you to move the boxes from the back of the store to the front, do you complain to him and put it off until later? Maybe you tell him all the reasons why the boxes should stay in the back of the store. And you expect him to cut you a paycheck? *Laziness, in essence, is when a person wants to be provided for without exerting self.* Don't let that be true of you. Earn your pay!

Lazy people go to sleep early at night then sleep late in the morning. "Laziness casts into a deep sleep, and an idle man will suffer hunger" (Proverbs 19:15, NASV). Go ahead and sleep, lazy person. Dream on about finding a lucrative job you can do from your laptop, pool-side at your twenty five room mansion. Then wake up to find yourself in poverty. "If you love sleep, you will end in poverty" (Proverbs 20:13.) Wake up and get to work! Lazy people are content just to be idle, doing nothing. You are different. Get your hands busy doing something productive!

"Lazy people consider themselves smarter than seven wise counselors" (Proverbs 26:16). Because they think they are smarter and more talented than others, lazy people are un-teachable. They tell themselves they should not have to work hard. Things should come to them with ease.

Last night, at about eight-thirty, Cheryl and I got back from supper with friends. The new season of *American Idol* was just starting, on the Hong Kong channel Star World. What fun! A few of those trying out actually had singing ability. They had obviously worked hard at learning to sing well before showing up in our living room. However, most of the people trying out definitely should not be singing on TV ever again! The odd thing is that some of them were so sure of their abilities, they already quit their day jobs! "Look at me everybody! I'm the next American Idol!" Don't deceive yourself. Intelligence and talent coming from a know-it-all couch potato will not be rewarded for very long at all.

There are three rewards that tend to come toward those who are not lazy.

- Growth as a Leader - "Work hard and become a leader; be lazy and become a slave" (Proverbs 12:24).
- Greater Income - "Lazy hands make a man poor, but diligent hands bring wealth" (Proverbs 10:4, NIV).
- Contentment - "Lazy people want much but get little, but those who work hard will prosper and be satisfied" (Proverbs 13:4). The greatest reward for not being lazy is personal satisfaction. You know you have done your best.

Ever notice that it's possible to be self-motivated about personal things but have no motivation on the job? Some people are lazy full-time. Others are just part-time lazy bums. When you are part-time lazy, it's time for an attitude check. Do you just *have* a job, or are you truly *thankful* to have a job? Are you thankful for your particular job? Right now, say to God, "Lord, my job is a gift from You. Thank You for giving it to me. From now on, I want You to help me do everyday business as Your business. Help me embrace my job with passion. Let my work be a blessing to my employer and to others." With that attitude, it will be very hard to be lazy. Laziness is just one reason why some people don't succeed in their careers. Here's another.

Lack of Career Focus

He who works his land will have abundant food, but he who chases fantasies lacks judgment. Proverbs 12:11 (NIV)

We've looked at the lazy person. Now here's a person not yet succeeding at a career for a different reason. This person is not lazy. He or she has ambition and motivation, but is lacking a clear career focus. This guy or gal is energetic, but just doesn't know what to do with all that nervous energy. So they go after kinds of work that just don't make any sense for who they are. "He who pursues vain things lacks sense" (Proverbs 12:11, NASV). This person sits on fertile land rich with potential income, and what does he do? He puts five thousand dollars down on an internet get-rich quick scheme. Sometimes we do not succeed at work simply because, even though we are surrounded with what ought to be obvious opportunities, we lack the focus to see them and stay with them. Instead, we follow worthless, trivial pursuits.

On the south shore of Hong Kong Island, we have seven beaches within twenty minutes of where we live. I love to swim far out into the ocean. Even in the winter time, it's great exercise, if you have a wet suit. A few weeks ago, I was enjoying a day of rest, riding my bike along the coast. Then out on the ocean I saw an old ship that looked like it belonged in a pirate movie. Wow! That ship was calling me to come out to it. So off the bike I went and into the water. I swam toward that ship for at least forty minutes. Finally, I pulled up beside it. Huge wood planks lined the deck of the old wooden ship. Tall, rough masts reached high into the sky. The dark, all wood vessel was about two hundred feet long. A few young men were working on board.

I called out to them in Chinese. "*Wo neng bu neng shang lai?*" ("Can I come up or not?")

They just looked down at me in the water, and then looked at each other. The look they gave each other said, "*Yo fong kuang de lau wei yau shang lai! Bu xing!*" ("There's some crazy white man from the other side of the world down there in the water!")

Most people actually like me when they first meet me, but to my surprise, those pirates didn't throw down a rope to let me on board! I had chased a fantasy. There was no going on board the pirate ship for this white man. Nothing to do but swim all the way back to shore without any rest! At least my bike was still there waiting on me.

Are you chasing after some fantasy of a dream job? Are you hoping that one day your ship will magically come into shore? The longer we pursue trivial vocations, the less discernment we develop, and the poorer we become. "The one who chases fantasies will have his fill of poverty" (Proverbs 28:19, NIV). Are you chasing after pirate ships? Your bike is still waiting on you, but it may not always be there. Unattended bikes have a way of disappearing. Get back to your bike. Focus on the possibilities right around you. Do you say, "If I could just find the right job, then life would be so much better?" That's chasing after pirate ships. *The real opportunity for success lies more within the person than it does in the job.* Bloom in the land where you are planted.

The wisdom coach says successful people keep their hand on the plow, working their own land. They find a vocational niche early in life and stick with it. They focus on something they are passionate about. Does that mean that you must become locked into doing only one thing all the rest of your life? Not at all! Land produces different things in different seasons. The land you own now can produce crops and give you abundant food. In a later season, oil may be discovered underneath your land, bringing you a monthly check. In still another season of life, you might build houses on your land and rent them out. By retirement time, you may have windmills producing electricity, or you might be raising buffalo on your land!

There are so many things you can do with the resources you already have. Do you recognize the land underneath you? What you recognize, you energize! Look at your hobbies, abilities, and relationships. What are the things you understand well? Those things are the land underneath you, just waiting to bless you into a God-designed career path. For those living vocationally "in the zone," one thing progresses to another. God directs life's seasons of work, each with its own skills, challenges, and rewards.

An eight year old boy named Truett saw people who were thirsty outdoors in his neighborhood. He bought drinks in bulk and sold them to those neighbors at a slight profit. He then bought newspapers in bulk, and delivered them punctually with a friendly smile. As a young man, Truett and his brother opened a small snack and coffee shop, with ten stools and four tables. The place was so small they called it "Dwarf Grill." They soon opened a location in a mall, and added a chicken steak sandwich, which became known as "Chick-fil-a."

Now a huge nation-wide chain, the company started by Truett Cathy provides university scholarships to employees, offers "Camp Winshape" for hundreds of at-risk children every summer, runs a dozen or more "Winshape Homes" for foster kids, and provides "Winshape Marriage Retreats" for missionaries around the world.[6] Truett found his "land": excellence in providing a product to meet the needs of people. He cultivated his land through seasons of providing beverages, newspapers, and chicken sandwiches, all the while making a spiritual impact on people. What a great legacy!

Stop being distracted by passing pirate ships out there in never-never land. Find the things around you that you can be passionate about, things that you can enjoy doing and already have a knack for doing. Look at what you enjoyed in high school. Ask your friends and family what they see you doing well as a career. Focus on those things for the general direction of your career track. Refuse to follow a frivolous get rich scheme that later makes you scream. It can lead you here and there, yet nowhere.

Are you drifting from one type of work to the next? Are you experiencing a failure to launch into your God-designed career path? Work your own land. Get a work focus that flows out of who you are and where you are, and stay with it! Don't worry about chasing more glamorous careers! Find the land under your feet, and cultivate it. That land will provide plenty of food for you and others, as God leads you through meaningful career seasons. Don't let a lack of career *focus* keep you from success in the work place.

Pride

Before his downfall, a man's heart is proud.
Proverbs 18:12 (NIV)

Now here's a person who is neither lazy nor unfocused, but is still failing at work. This person is failing because of arrogance, or haughtiness. This is the guy who just loves to strut his stuff! My Dad would say he's "too big for his britches!" Though pride brings a twisted and temporary satisfaction, it is the very opposite of honoring God. God hates a proud look (see Proverbs 16:16–17).

What problems are caused by pride on the job? Because of pride, we pretend to be someone we're not. "One man pretends to be rich, yet has nothing" (Proverbs 13:7, NIV). What a tiring lifestyle! When we are placed with others on a team at work, pride causes us to have serious relational challenges. A prideful leader controls others. Prideful followers rebel against authority. With pride, we compete instead of cooperate. Instead of contributing, we are contrary. "Pride leads to arguments" (Proverbs 13:10). Instead of looking out for the common good, when we operate in pride we look out for number one. Instead of promoting the product, the prideful person seeks self promotion. "It is not good for people to think about all the honors they deserve" (Proverbs 25:27). It takes a downfall, like getting fired, before a person can come to grips with his own prideful heart.

W.A. Criswell, the legendary pastor of First Baptist Church of Dallas, kept a beautifully bound book by his desk titled "My Humility and How I Achieved It." Were you to open the book, you would find it full of over two hundred pages, all completely blank! We are all prideful. If you are proud of how humble you are, then you are not humble! What is pride? It's when you "look in the mirror to find the source of all success and out the window for the cause of all failure."[7] People who are full of themselves don't last long at one job site.

While serving in Korea as missionaries for twelve years, Cheryl and I had many unusual opportunities beyond sharing the gospel, helping start churches, and training Koreans going out as missionaries. As foreigners who spoke the language, we found ourselves, like it or not, living a life of some notoriety. Talk show hosts of national TV and radio shows had us on the air to be interviewed. Cheryl and I sang together several times in Korean for the nationally televised New Year's Day celebration. It was difficult to go anywhere without being recognized and talked about.

Looking back on those years, I am filled with gratitude for Koreans who humbly worked behind the scenes, so that we could serve the Lord in their land. Deacon Han comes to mind. He never appeared on anybody's TV show. Tirelessly and humbly, he worked so diligently to serve the needs of missionaries. He always wanted to know if there was anything he could do to help us.

There was nothing in it for Deacon Han. No chance of climbing the ladder. No glory. No gold. There was nothing, except the satisfaction of helping others. I watched Deacon Han care for missionaries day after day, year after year. He went on long road trips to get what missionaries needed, sometimes even sleeping in his car. Never once did I see in him any self-serving, prideful spirit. It's no wonder that Deacon Han was able to hold down the same job for decades, and enjoy his work. In January 2002, as he was helping us pack up to move to a Mandarin speaking area, cancer overcame him quickly, and Deacon Han was given rest from his faithful, humble service. He went to be with the Lord. Few people I have known have genuine humility like Deacon Han.

Pride is one reason for job failure. There is another reason for lack of success on the job.

Greed

A greedy person tries to get rich quick, but it only leads to poverty. Proverbs 28:22

Another reason why some people cannot seem to find satisfaction at the work place is their own uncontrolled appetite for more and more. Greed is a condition that can afflict a person regardless of how much money he or she has, or doesn't have. What happens when a greedy person is a part of the work mix? "Greed causes fighting" (Proverbs 28:25). On the job, a greedy person will compete with others. He or she will work things around so that self gains more than others and more than the organization. Conflict is inevitable. If we trust in self to provide our needs, we will always scramble to survive. Self-centered gain is no gain at all. "Those who are stingy will lose everything" (Proverbs 11:24).

Want to become more valuable to your company? Add more value to your company through selflessness. Give yourself away. The only way to be consistently selfless is to rely on God to provide the things you truly need. Only when you trust in the Lord will your restless pursuit of more and more finally come to an end. Find your satisfaction in your Creator. He will never disappoint. Greed will never satisfy. Regardless of what you have, it's never enough.

In all of our years overseas, we have had a local person working in our home, helping us with language, child care, grocery shopping, cooking, and cleaning. Full time language study initially required us to have a house helper. We soon discovered that house helpers are great interpreters of life for us, helping us to be able to relax knowing that a local person is watching out for us. Without a helper, we would be paying the foreigner's price for groceries–about twenty percent more than what the locals negotiate.

Our employment of a helper has turned out to be a very positive experience almost every time. We have found locals to be trustworthy, hardworking, caring, and smart. Only once was this not true. When Mrs. "Shi" came to work for us, we had eight sets of dishes. Occasionally she would report to us that some dishes broke. She said she threw them away. Soon we were down to only four sets, one set for each of the four of us in our family. Dishes never "broke" after that. We thought it was strange but decided not to make an issue of it. Then towels started disappearing. At the suggestion of local friends, we asked Mrs. "Shi" if she had misplaced the towels. She said she might have. Within a few days, they found their way back to us.

We left a key to the house for Mrs. "Shi" while we went on vacation. When we got back, we noticed that Cheryl's heirloom gold and diamond jewelry, valued at several thousand dollars, was gone. After we questioned her, Mrs. "Shi" finally wept out a confession, saying she sold the jewelry for cash to pay for her son's higher education. Shortly after that, her son got in a fist fight, was detained by authorities and hospitalized, only to die from resulting injuries. There is nothing good to gain from greed. Don't let it be a part of who you are.

We've looked at four reasons why some people struggle to find and hold down a job that they are passionate about. Some people sabotage their own careers with laziness, a lack of clear vocational focus, pride, and greed. Those are proven ways to fail at work. Now let's look at how to do well in your career.

HOW TO SUCCEED AT WORK

Work Hard

Good planning and hard work lead to prosperity, but hasty shortcuts lead to poverty. Proverbs 21:5

The lazy wait for a money making idea to zap them in the forehead. The wise pick up the plow. Many people spend much energy just trying to figure out how to keep from working. The wise person knows the value and benefits of hard work. "Hard workers have plenty of food; playing around brings poverty" (Proverbs 28:19). Hard work generally results in profit for the company (14:23), personal increase in wealth (12:11, 10:4), satisfaction (13:4), and an easier path through life (15:19). What is involved in working hard? Don't assume you know the answer. Consider the following facets of hard work carefully, and evaluate your own work habits. How should you work hard?

Be Persistent. "The desires of the diligent are fully satisfied" (Proverbs 13:4, NIV). If at first you don't succeed, welcome to the human race. You're just like most people. Those who fail give up after one try. Don't give up. Try again, but this time, make some changes in your approach. Remember, God wants us to triumph at work. Try. Then if you fail, try again, adding some more "umph." Triumph!

Diligence pays off. "Due diligence" is the buzz word around the Central District of Hong Kong, where international business people control billions of dollars worth of world trade. These people know the importance of sweating the little details. Our church here in Hong Kong is full of such CEOs. They have developed the ability to keep at something difficult until it is achieved. Diligence is part of what helped them arrive at the rewarding positions they now hold.

You don't have to be a graying, Hong Kong world class executive to learn diligence. You may be a university student on summer break. "A wise youth works hard all summer" (Proverbs 10:5, NIV). Few things come easy in life, but persistence will get you there. Young person, you are a part of a generation that seldom has an opportunity to do hard work. Your grandparents lived on a farm, and knew all about milking the cows at five in the morning. They walked five miles to and from school, barefoot in the snow, uphill both directions. However, your generation is largely urbanized, and that's okay. You don't have to apologize for not being born in a barn. You are more familiar with graffiti than you are with grunt work. It is my prayer that you discover the delight of hard work, the satisfaction of mastering a craft, and the joy of providing for others. Find work that you can enjoy, and do it diligently, with gusto. I dare you to graffiti this slogan on the walls of your brain: "Diligent hands will rule" (Proverbs 12:24, NIV).

During his university days, a young man named Mark started collecting touching stories. He began sharing these stories with others. People paid attention to his stories, so he and a friend decided to try to publish them. However, the book of heart-touching, soul penetrating stories was turned down by thirty three publishers, and then by more than a hundred publishers at a book fair. They all said, "A book of soppy stories will never sell." Finally a publisher in Florida said they would print, if Mark and his friend Jack would buy the first twenty thousand copies with their own money! They decided to do it. Mark Victor Hansen and Jack

Canfield have since seen more than thirty million copies of their soppy stories sold, in one form or another, of *Chicken Soup for the Soul.*[8] Work with persistence. It's good for the soul, and it certainly isn't bad for the pocket book either.

Be resourceful. "Lazy people don't even cook the game they catch, but the diligent make use of everything they find" (Proverbs 12:27). American Indians made use of nearly every part of the buffalo. Bones were chiseled into arrows and cooking utensils. Internal chambers of the animal were cleaned and used like we use zip lock bags today. Learn to creatively use all resources available. Want to succeed on the job? Seek out and discover resources in unusual places, and use them in out-of-the box ways to get the task done. Get the job done with less.

If you understand your work from only one angle, then you do not understand it at all. Turn the work around in your mind to see it from a different point of view. Take, for example, an international fashion design company with which I am connected. The company was just about to go under financially, when a resourceful innovation saved it. The leaders looked at their business from all directions. They thought of the buyers of their dresses, the shops that sell their garments, the market niche for such garments, the availability of the required fabric, the labor needed to make the garment, and the relationships with all those involved. Each facet of the work required certain resources. In this case, the making of the garment in a factory owned by the fashion company was eating up all their funds. The solution? Sell the factory and outsource the garment making to small shops and people who could make the dresses in their homes. The company is now rebuilding based on the innovation. They are working hard by using out-of-the-box resources.

Be self-motivated. "Take a lesson from the ants, you lazy bones. Learn from their ways and be wise! Even though they have no prince, governor, or ruler to make them work, they labor hard all summer, gathering food for the winter" (Proverbs 6:6–8). Look at the ants. No one has to crack a whip over them to get them moving. No supervisor ant comes along beside them and offers a pay raise or an office with a view. Something within those ants keeps them working hard.

I recently took in a Thailand mountain trail with some friends. We had thrown a football around in a clear spot of land, and then sat down under a pavilion. Someone had dropped some potato chips on the ground. A stream of ants was rapidly taking those potato chips home to feed their big family. We were amazed at how the ants worked together. No sergeant was barking orders at them to motivate them. Then suddenly they marched straight into a wall. "Dumb ants; can't even see a wall right in front of them!" We thought the wall would bring frustration and confusion. Not at all! What did those ants do? Knowing exactly where they were going, they turned and marched straight up that wall, carrying huge potato chips fifty times their size.

The first few inches straight up were extremely slow going. Gravity was working so hard against them that soon they were actually moving backwards instead of forwards. Then they found that extra "umph" needed to get the chips moving upward again. None of them quit. Here is how the conversation *didn't* go. One ant says, "This level of work wasn't in my contract." His buddy replies, "Yeah. I didn't sign up for this!" And another says, "Better give me double pay!"

The wisdom coach wants us to take a lesson from the ant. Don't let your bones get lazy. Even when no one is micro-managing you, work hard. Work with excellence. When the laws of nature seem to be pulling against you, pull together with others and give it all you've got. "If you fail under pressure, your strength is not very great" (Proverbs 24:10).

Let work pressures bring out the best in you, motivating you even more.

Be a team player. "An unfriendly man pursues selfish ends" (Proverbs 18:1, NIV). Ants know how to work together. People who fail at completing a task are those that ask, "What can *I* do?" They look only at their own resources and abilities, not at the whole picture. What limits them is their self-centered approach to getting the job done. The mantra of this generation seems to be, "Have faith in yourself. It's all about me. I am self-sufficient. I alone will get it done my way. Then I will get all the credit for this job." The result is that gravity pulls the potato chip down off the work wall. You can't hold up the work by yourself. "He who trusts in himself is a fool" (Proverbs 28:26, NIV). What does the successful, wise person do? He or she asks, "What's it going to take to get it done?" Then the hard worker mobilizes people and resources to defy gravity. One ant by himself cannot do it.

Many young people today are considering becoming missionaries. The desire is noble. However, as I have taught in seminaries and mentored those who want to serve the Lord overseas, I have noticed a disturbing trend. Young people want to go to the mission field to use a specific skill they have. They see mission service as a way to further develop their individual gifts and abilities. After they arrive on the field, they find that above all, team work is the main thing required of them. A tension develops between doing their own thing and being a team player. Some insist on doing their own thing, only to discover that their skill is not what reaches the local people. They don't feel valued or needed, and leave the mission field frustrated. Others decide it's not about what self can do. It's about doing whatever it takes to reach people. Those are the ones who develop new skills, grow as people, and become great team players.

A successful worker does not start with self. He or she starts with the goal that needs to be reached. The individual ants don't find the potato chip, sit down, and feed their faces. Imagine the reaction of the other ants to such a self centered ant. "Hey, get up! This is not about you! This is about the good of the colony! The goal here is to store up food for the whole colony for the winter. If you just want to sit here feeding your own fat face while we do all the hard work hauling our food supply, we're taking that chip from you and heading home without you. You'll be getting very hungry out here on your own! Get up and work together to get these potato chips home...NOW!" The goal is the colony. As believers, our goal is the Kingdom of God. Regardless of our profession, we work for the King and His glory, not for the sake of feeding our own faces, or developing our own selves. Are you a kingdom team player?

Working hard involves being a persistent, resourceful, self-motivated, team player. Does that describe you? Now here's the second step toward success at work.

Work Smart.

Know the state of your flocks, and put your heart into caring for your herds, for riches don't last forever, and the crown might not be secure for the next generation. After the hay is harvested, the new crop appears, and the mountain grasses are gathered in, your sheep will provide wool for clothing, and you goats will be sold for the price of a field. And you will have enough goats' milk for you, your family, and your servants.
Proverbs 27:23-27

Don't just work hard. Work smart. Your employer doesn't just want sweat. He or she wants results. If you have your own business, you don't want to put in the longest hours possible at the job site. You want to get the work done as efficiently as possible so you can say "well done," then go home and enjoy your family. Notice specific ways our wisdom coach tells us to work smart.

Know the answers to the questions "What is my business?" and "How's business?" The wisdom coach says "know the state of your flocks." What is the business in this case study? It is flocks of animals. What does the coach command this goat rancher to do? He is to know the state of his business. Can you state simply what your business is? If you don't know your target, how will you hit it? Work on a simple, clear definition of what your business is. Let that definition include why you are in the business. For example, a landlord might say, "In order to give working families a nice place to live, we provide affordable, quality, single family rental housing at approximately 95% of market price."

To know the state of the flocks, the rancher must not merely rely on reports from his workers. He must go out to the fields and see first-hand whether or not those sheep are bleating happily. In the case of a landlord, he must not merely receive the monthly report from the property manager, stating that all eleven of his houses are currently occupied. He must go see the conditions of those houses, meet those who are living in them, and ask them what their needs are. What is your business? How is business?

Emotionally invest in your work. "Put your heart into caring for your herds" (Proverbs 27:23). Do you know your sheep by name? Do they know that you care? If you have lost your love for your work, you may be burned out. Take a full two week vacation away somewhere without work e-mail.

Pray, asking God to renew your passion for your work. Look at changes that might need to be made in what you are doing, the way you are doing it, or who you are doing it with. Take a look at how your work may be negatively impacting your spirit and your family. What should be done about that? If after doing all that, you are still not passionate about your work, it may be time to consider what you *could* be passionate about doing. Just make it something tied to who and where you are. No need to chase after pirate ships!

Remember, success without succession is failure. "The crown might not be secure for the next generation" (Proverbs 27:24). Though in your life-time you may succeed and enjoy a fairly royal life, don't assume that you will automatically benefit those who come after you. Work strategically with a long range plan of how your work and life will help those you leave behind. How are you raising up future leaders? How are you working to communicate biblical values to your children, grandchildren, and those you mentor at work and within your church? What does your will look like? Is it how you want it? If you do not continue to closely monitor your financial and relational investments, your wealth can disappear quickly. When the seasons of your own vocation change, who are you preparing to take over your current work? Successful people have a succession plan.

Capitalize on the rhythmic cycle of your occupation. Proverbs gives us a picture of a rancher harvesting hay at the time it is ready. He stockpiles it as future food for his livestock. While he does so, he notices the new grass growing for the next season. Want to be successful at work? Pay attention to the seasonal nature of your work. Develop the art of keeping track of many projects at once, each in a different stage of development. Work on current projects, while at the same time following through with previous projects, and preparing for what's next. Get the seasonal nature of your work going in your favor. Doing so requires skill development. What help do you need to seek out, in order to develop particular skill areas? What cycle of your occupation is most difficult for you? Seek out the help you need in that area. Ask your boss for the opportunity to be trained in those skills.

End-vision your work. "Your sheep will provide wool for clothing, and your goats will be sold for the price of a field" (Proverbs 27:26). Now those are some valuable goats! Set goals that help motivate you to be the best manager possible of your work. Have the end in mind from the beginning. Keep a vision before you of the clothing-making parties you're going to have when the sheep are sheared. Be ready to sell the sheep, and then follow through with your plan to buy another field for expanding next season. Be smart about how you use your profits. Reinvest them back into business growth. Use them for the benefit of your family, and the development of your people. "You will have enough goats' milk for you, your family, and your servants" (Proverbs 27:27).

Recognize that the harvest is from God. Is the farmer the one who made the grass grow? Is he the one who caused the sheep to multiply? The wisdom coach gives us a picture of man and God working together to see a good harvest. Sure, the man did his part, otherwise there would have been no harvest. However, it is clearly God who is acknowledged as the primary Partner. One hospital administrator often felt pressure about decisions needing to be made. He developed the habit of keeping an empty chair in his office. If anyone attempted to sit in that chair, he would say "Sorry, that chair is occupied." He thought of it as the "Jesus Chair," and it was the best chair in his office. He was constantly reminded that Jesus was there with him, giving him wisdom, peace, humility, and confidence to do his job. "Whoever keeps the fig tree will eat its fruit; so he who waits on his master will be honored" (Proverbs 27:18, NKJV).

Work with Integrity.

People with integrity have firm footing, but those who follow crooked paths will slip and fall. People who wink at wrong cause trouble. Proverbs 10:9-10

You will *often* see good results from working hard. There will *normally* be benefits from working smart. In the end you will *always* reap what your character sows. Even the best work done in the smartest way can fall flat. Why so? If the path taken so diligently and smartly was a curvy, crooked path, you will spin out going around a corner too fast. You will slip and fall.

You may be saying "Not if I don't get caught!" I have news for you. You are caught each moment of your life. You cannot escape the eyes of God. He sees all you do. He knows all you think. Don't wink at wrong. Don't think it's daring to see what you can get away with at work. That's not daring. That's dumb. Sure you can take or give a bribe, but is it the right thing to do? You can gather receipts to turn in on things you didn't really pay for, and get reimbursed for more than you paid. But is it the right thing to do?

There are some jobs that are very lucrative but are not to be done by a person of integrity. You can set up a gambling casino. That will give you a large profit from people who have nothing better to do with their money than feed it into a machine, but is it the right thing to do? You can set up a sweat shop and hire illegal immigrants, paying them a mere fraction of what others would require. Your profits would soar, but is it the right thing to do? You could work at a financial firm and gain insight useful in insider trading, but is it the right thing to do? God is looking for men and women who will stand tall in the workplace, high above the moral fog of our day. He wants us to be trustworthy workers, doing what is right on the job.

"The trustworthy will get a rich reward" (Proverbs 28:20). Look at the benefits of working with integrity:

- A firm vocational foundation - "People with integrity have firm footing" (Proverbs 10:9). You are a person working in ways and industries that show integrity, and God is eager to bless you by causing you to be well established in your career.
- A clear guidance system - "The integrity of the upright will guide them" (Proverbs 11:3, NASV). Decisions become much easier for you because you no longer ask, "What's the best choice for my gain?" Instead you simply ask, "What is the right thing to do?"
- A blessed family life– "The godly walk with integrity; blessed are their children after them" (Proverbs 20:7). You come home with inner peace from having done the right thing at work. Your peace blesses your family.
- A favored position with both God and man– "Do not let kindness and truth leave you; Bind them around your neck, Write them on the tablet of your heart. So you will find favor and good repute in the sight of God and man" (Proverbs 3:3–4 NASV). You know that life is about developing character through

living out God's truth. You are doing so and thus gaining the respect of men and the pleasure of God.

- A sense of wholeness–The word "integrity," used in Proverbs, means "complete." A life of integrity has all parts of the person living in accord with each other. Wholeness is not experienced by the one who on Sunday professes to live for God, but then leaves church to live for self during the week.

James H. Amos, Jr. is president of Mail Boxes, Etc. Among the top 500 franchises, *Entrepeneur* magazine ranks Mail Boxes, Etc. number one in the business service category, a position it has held for a decade. Now CEO for more than 12,000 employees, James says, "I look for people who have good character first, then competence in their discipline. You can train and teach the skill. It's much more difficult to instill character and integrity into someone."

How did his spiritual life begin? While serving our country in Vietnam, he searched for answers. Then after returning to the U.S. as a former marine, he says, "I bowed my head at my desk one day and asked the Lord Jesus into my life. That's when I began this journey, this lifelong process of learning to live by God's principles...I can't separate Sunday from the rest of the week, nor do I believe I should."[9] Everyday work done with integrity blesses self and others. The only way to be working out of a heart that consistently desires to do the right thing is to have a new heart. The ones we are born with are prone to do what's best for self. You are not capable of changing your heart or giving yourself a new one. Jesus is the heart specialist. Let Him give you a new heart. With His heart within you, a life of integrity in the workplace is possible.

SPEAK WORDS OF BLESSING!

Enjoying the Positive Results of Your Words

In the early 1990's, Pastor Song invited us to help start a new church in a new satellite city near Seoul. The new city, called Boondang, is one of more than a dozen planned cities absorbing the population growth of Korea's expanding capitol. One day in Boondang, a wealthy church family had us over for a special meal. When we arrived, we slipped our shoes off at the door, as is the custom. We sat on the immaculately clean floor and breathed in an array of aromas drifting into the living room from the kitchen. Soon, a beautiful wooden table was brought to where we were sitting. The table was carved with symbols of blessings, set in the deep grain of rich wood. The height was just right for sitting on the floor with our legs crossed underneath the table, and our arms and mouths above it.

An assortment of small dishes, called *panchan,* were placed on the table, These included dried minnows (*myeulchi*), spicy fermented cabbage called *kimchi,* seaweed, octopus, raw oysters, and other expensive delicacies. We each used chopsticks to move the food from the dishes in the middle of the table straight into our mouths. There were no individual plates or serving utensils. All of this required a broadening of our perspective, but what had we come half way around the world for, if we were not willing to eat the food of the local people? After trying each dish, we found them quite delicious. It's nearly two decades later now, and can you guess what my wife Cheryl put in my stocking this past Christmas? *Myeulchi!* I opened my stocking at about seven in the morning, and by midmorning both packets of dried minnows were already devoured! I tried keeping them all to myself, but the family overpowered me. Don't be deceived by our appearance: we are *not* typical Americans!

Let's get back to that meal in Boondang. The main course came out next. The usual polite excuses were made by the hostess. "This is just something simple we put together, and it may not be very good, but we hope you like it." A large burner was placed in the middle of the table, then a hot pot full of vegetables, meat, and spices was placed on the burner's open flame.

"This looks delicious. What is it?"

"*Poshintang,*" was the proud reply. We had never had that before, nor had we even heard of it.

"What does '*poshintang*' mean?"

"It is a special winter-time meal that gives you vitality and warmth. *Poshintang* means soup that protects your health."

So we ate to our health. The meat tasted very good. Obviously, much effort had been put into getting the spice mix just right. The taste reminded me of the wild deer I had eaten in East Texas. Our hostess said the leafy green vegetables, cooked with the meat, helped absorb odor and balance the taste. I began to worry. What kind of animal needed something to absorb the odor of its meat?

That soup tasted so good. Even though it was the noon meal, I ate so much that I didn't need to eat again until the next day! After lunch, I asked our hostess what kind of meat is used in *poshintang*. When I heard the answer, I thought it was a joke, but quickly realized it was not.

"*Poshintang* is made from only the finest selection of specially bred Korean dogs!"

We looked at each other, and without saying a word, our eyes said to each other, "What? We have been gorging ourselves on dog meat? What would our American friends have to say about this? This is definitely *not* something we're going to ever put in print somewhere! (Which means that you, reader, must promise me you won't ever show this book to anyone else!) What do we say to this Korean lady who fed us dog soup without telling us what it was?"

We had already eaten the dog soup. We didn't want to say the wrong thing, then have to eat our words as well. Our hostess was feeling that she had honored us by what she had done. She had served us a very expensive meal reserved for special guests on rare occasions. We were feeling like she had tricked us, but the worst thing was that some poor dog had given his life so we could eat him for lunch! What do we say to the lady who did this to us?

So many times in life we don't know what to say. What are the words appropriate for such a situation? Too often we respond thoughtlessly and then wish we could take back what we have said. It's no fun saying something, only to quickly regret what came out of your mouth. Eating your words is not a pleasant diet. "The babbling of a fool invites trouble" (Proverbs 10:14).

If we use our mouth in destructive ways, we are bringing about our own destruction (see Proverbs 10:14, 10:31). Speaking harmful words and expecting it not to hurt you is like lighting a cherry bomb between your own lips and being surprised when it blows your mouth apart. Think of the problems a motor mouth can create–

- hastily making promises that cannot be kept.
- losing income due to a loose mouth. "Work brings profit, but mere talk leads to poverty" (Proverbs 14:23).
- releasing private information.
- responding to hurtful words with even more hurt.
- twisting the truth to imply things that may not be true.
- needlessly offending others.
- spouting out a solution before knowing what the problem is. "What a shame, what folly, to give advice before listening to the facts" (Proverbs 18:13)!

Although our goal is positive benefits from speech that blesses others, you can see just how far away we are from that goal. How can we possibly enjoy positive benefits from the words we say when there tends to be so much negativity coming out of our mouths? Let's first take a look at verbal habits that need to be stopped. Once we deal with these negative verbal habits, we will then be able to focus on new ways of speech that bless others.

HOW TO AVOID EATING YOUR WORDS

Here's how to avoid taking back what you say. Follow these principles, and you won't regret what you have said. The first principle may be the toughest one!

Keep your mouth shut!

Don't talk too much, for it fosters sin. Be sensible and turn off the flow! Proverbs 10:21

Excessive words get us in trouble! Do you find yourself saying, "Well, I haven't given that much thought, but just off the top of my head...blah, blah, blah..." You know what comes off the top of your head? Dandruff!

Some people have more verbal ability than others. Each believer has received at least one spiritual gift at salvation. Some have the gift of serving. others have the gift of leadership, and so forth. Some of us run at the mouth as if we have the gift of gab! Although our culture idolizes the extrovert, the wisdom coach says having a natural tendency toward being talkative actually is *not* an asset. It is not a gift from God. Talkativeness is a verbal liability. Follow the golden rule: silence is golden!

"Wise people don't make a show of their knowledge, but fools broadcast their folly" (Proverbs 12:23). Those who talk the most have the least to say. If you don't really have anything to say, please don't give us verbal evidence to prove it! There is no need to broadcast your ignorance. Excessive talk is just gobbledygook that makes people's ears tired. Don't mouth off mindlessly. "If you keep your mouth shut, you will stay out of trouble" (Proverbs 21:23). You never have to explain what you never say. "A truly wise person uses few words" (Proverbs 17:27).

Your mouth is a door to your heart. Place a spam filter at your mouth. When junk messages are attempting to come out, the guard will delete them before they are sent. Have the guard notify the Control Panel, who is the Holy Spirit. The guard says, "Spirit, this heart has issues. It's leaky. Things are always trying to spew up from it and out of the mouth. This heart needs You to do Your work. Find out what's down there keeping things all stirred up and spewing out. This heart is still not resting calmly."[10]

Do you want to stop having to eat your own words? Then you must first learn to keep your mouth shut. What else must you do?

Stop Launching Verbal Missiles.

Reckless words pierce like a sword.
Proverbs 12:18 (NIV)

Our society tells us it's cool to cut down other people. Just how popular is it to insult others and make rude remarks? I just did a web search for "insults." There were 14,200,000 sites to choose from! Many of these sites brag about how well they can help you develop the art of saying cruel things to those who "deserve it." I opened a few of the sites and was tempted to quote some of what I saw there in order to give you examples of verbal insults. But I just couldn't do it. I don't want those kinds of words in a book with my name on it. You've heard enough examples from daily life. You know what harsh words sound like.

Is it really an asset to learn how to shoot verbal missiles at others? The wisdom coach tells us clearly: if you hurl verbal spears at others, it is a liability, not an asset. Listen with wise ears to what is said on the TV sitcoms. Much of what is pushed as funny is actually verbal cruelty. You choose to tune your TV and radio to the things that are on your heart. Is there some re-tuning needed in your heart?

Our society values quick wit and a destructive tongue. The person who can instantly respond to an insult with an even greater insult is seen as highly intelligent. If you are verbally slow, chances are you see your lack of ability to quickly hurl back an insult as a liability. The truth is that you are blessed. Your verbal slowness is an asset. The wisdom coach says, "A quick retort can ruin everything" (Proverbs 13:3).

Cruel cut-downs are so much a part of American chatter. What should you do when someone in the group cuts down someone else and expects you to laugh? You may be surprised that the Bible gives a clear answer. "Wrongdoers listen to wicked talk; liars pay attention to destructive words" (Proverbs 17:4). What should you do? Refuse to listen. Is it time to resensitize your ears? Do not allow the spam messages of cruelty into your inbox. Mark them as junk, and delete them automatically.

Train your tongue! Take a look at the messages in your verbal outbox–messages that you speak to others. Though it may make you feel powerful to launch verbal attack missiles that hurt others, what kind of person does that make you? Is that really who you want to become? Have you hurt someone with your words? Go to them and ask forgiveness.

Refuse to accept hurtful words as normal or funny. Don't respond to hurtful words with words that cut even deeper. When you are insulted, respond with kindness. "A gentle answer turns away wrath, but harsh words stir up anger" (Proverbs 15:1).

Are you with me so far? What are the first two habits that will keep you from having to eat your words? Did you reply with "Keep your mouth shut. Stop launching verbal missiles"? Good! Here's a third verbal habit.

Don't let your tongue twist the truth.

"The twisted tongue tumbles into trouble." Proverbs 17:20

Try saying this faster and faster five times: "The twisted tongue tumbles into trouble." That's a real tongue twister! A crooked or perverted heart gets our tongue all twisted around, and results in self destruction. Avoid distorting the truth to achieve selfish ends.

Let's suppose that when you are parking your car, you slightly scrape the side of a Porsche SUV. You look around. No one is aware of what happened. The damage to the Porsche is minor, especially in comparison to its 70,000 dollar value. Would you leave a note to notify the owner of your name and number, *or* would you think that someone who owns that Porsche Cayenne must have plenty of money to fix a scratch from your Ford Tortoise?

There was a man who actually did scrape the side of a new Porsche, except people were watching. He took out a piece of paper and he wrote on it, "A number of people around me think I'm leaving you a note that includes my name and address, but I'm not."[11]

Sometimes it seems like the only way out of a tight situation is twisting the truth. Why are we prone to distort the truth? Deceitful words come from a desire for personal gain. Telling the truth can be expensive, but that's what becoming a person of integrity is all about–doing the right thing regardless of the cost. "It is better to be poor than dishonest" (Proverbs 19:22). The truth will eventually pay long term dividends back to you, but deceit is like a credit card. It makes you feel like you got something for nothing, but then it takes from you way more than it gives you. "Truthful lips will be established forever, but a lying tongue is only for a moment. Deceit is in the heart of those who devise evil" (Proverbs 12:19–20 NASV).

The wisdom coach piles on warning after warning to keep us from becoming liars. "Here is a description of worthless and wicked people: They are constant liars" (Proverbs 6:12). "Wealth created by lying is a vanishing mist and a deadly trap" (Proverbs 21:6). "A false witness will not go unpunished, nor will a liar escape" (Proverbs 19:5). "Lying lips are an abomination to the Lord, but those who deal faithfully are His delight" (Proverbs 12:22 NASV).

There is a fourth key to avoid eating your own words.

Refuse to Spread Gossip.

A perverse man spreads strife, and a slanderer separates intimate friends. Proverbs 16:28 (NASV)

There are those whose personal pain has led them beyond babbling unnecessarily, poking fun at others, or twisting the truth. Hurting people hurt people. Troubled people sometimes intentionally assassinate the character of others. They go around spreading harmful information to hurt someone else. Attacking the reputation of others by spreading gossip about them is not only wrong, it is cruel.

A few years ago here in Hong Kong, people were catching a terrible air borne disease called SARS. Panic struck the entire city, keeping people at home unless they absolutely had to go out. Those who did venture out were unfriendly to others, wore surgical masks on their faces, and sprayed elevator buttons with disinfectant before touching them. Some were even wearing swimming goggles!

During SARS, I had to go into the hospital to have back surgery. A car accident had broken my back, requiring titanium poles to be placed in my lower back bones. Hospitals were the one place where no one dared to go. You can imagine how thankful I was for the risk my wife and my dad took to stay with me in the hospital while the SARS epidemic was breaking out.

Professionals set about to determine how the disease was spreading, and they found out that the actual number of people who were spreading the disease was very low. Nevertheless, those who spread it were infecting very large numbers of people. These disease dispersers became known as super-spreaders.

What do you do about someone you don't like? Leave it to the immature and perverse to publicize negative things about others. Gossipers are sly super spreaders of verbal disease. You have better things to do with your words.

A lady was jealous of another female at church who seemed to be more beautiful and popular. In an attempt to tarnish the other lady's high profile image, the jealous woman began dishing out as "prayer requests" delicious morsels of gossip. Later she became consumed with guilt about what she had done, and went to her pastor to confess.

"Is it possible for me to make right what wrong I have done?" she asked.

"There are two things I want you to do before I answer,"

said the wise pastor. "Follow me." He led her to the church trash dumpster, pulled out a big bag of trash, and put it into her arms. "Go and spread this garbage all over town, then come back and see me."

The lady thought it was very strange, but she did as she was told, dumping pieces of the trash here and there all over town. Then she returned to the pastor's office.

"I did as you said."

"Good. Now will you do the second thing? Go back and collect all that trash."

"There's no telling where the wind has blown all the garbage I've spread all over town."

The pastor didn't say a word. He just looked at her for a long while in order to let her own words sink in.

"What dainty morsels rumors are-but they sink deep into one's heart" (Proverbs 18:8). Sometimes we latch onto a kind of food we just love to eat. Like a three year old boy plastering cake all over his face to get some of it in his mouth, we "feed our faces" faster and faster, not able to get enough of it. For some it's ice cream. For others it's one of the "basic" food groups, like chocolate. When we eat that food, we forget all about whether it's healthy food or junk food.

Gossip is something that people often love to take in, usually refusing to distinguish whether it is wholesome or not. In fact, just as junk food tastes better, gossip is more interesting than straight, boring facts. Healthy food processes well through your body and gives you energy. Junk food just turns into fat, triples in size, and hangs forever on your waist and hips. The dainty morsels of gossip do the same. They sink deep into your heart and become a long-term question mark about the character of the one who was slandered. The gossip and slander you hear get into your memory and mess with your mind.

What then should you do when a super spreader comes to you spouting off air-borne disease about someone? Put on your SARS mask! Get those goggles on, spray them with disinfectant, and leave the scene! Seriously, don't take in the garbage they are dishing out! "A gossip tells secrets, so don't hang around with someone who talks too much" (Proverbs 20:19). "Fire goes out for lack of fuel, and quarrels disappear when gossip stops" (Proverbs 26:20).

There are some misguided souls who are self appointed policemen of righteousness, feeling that the right thing to do is discover the faults of others and let them be known. Such a person is living life against the grain of God's grace. God says "Disregarding another person's faults preserves love; telling about them separates close friends" (Proverbs 17:9).

How do we go about using our speech to preserve love? First, we must take out of our verbal portfolio all of the liabilities we have just looked at. Be done with excessive talk, cutting down others, lying, and gossip. With all those bad habits done away with, what will we have left to say? What verbal assets should we then put into the vacuum created? How can we speak words that bless others, and enjoy the positive benefits of words well said? How do we speak words that feed the soul?

HOW TO SPEAK WORDS THAT FEED THE SOUL

I implore you. *Become a person who brings to the ears of others verbal gifts of life, healing, encouragement, and wisdom.* Those are the kind of words that people latch onto. We all like hearing uplifting words. "The words of the godly are like sterling silver" (Proverbs 10:20). People seek out those who bless others with positive words. Ask yourself this question: "Would others say that my words usually lift them up or bring them down?" Are your words like the wind that blows in their sail, moving them forward, or are your words like an anchor that pulls them down? Verbally bless others, and watch them blossom before your eyes. "Good people enjoy the positive results of their words" (Proverbs 13:2). There are four kinds of verbal gifts your words should be giving to others.

Speak Life!

The mouth of the righteous is a fountain of life.
Proverbs 10:11 (NASV)

When our lives are tapped into the river of living water flowing from the source of all life, then our words become to others refreshing vitality. In a verbal desert where the scorching heat of cutting words saps life out of the soul, where negative speech brings slow death to the spirit, a fountain of fresh, clean water springs up and gives strength. The words of those who walk with God speak life into others.

Our words are to speak life like a refreshing fountain. Learn to speak words that bless others at their point and time of need. Cultivate the art of knowing how and when to speak life to those who have something to celebrate, a loss to grieve, a joy to express, or a pain to share. There is someone in your path today waiting for you to speak life. Will you speak life to that one?

The only way that we can pour out the water of life to others is by having deep reserves within ourselves. Our words are to speak life to others from a deep reservoir within us. "A person's words can be life-giving water" (Proverbs

18:4). “The words of a man’s mouth are deep waters” (Proverbs 18:4, NIV). Our walk with God should cause us to be like an abundant and deep well of refreshing water, ready with ample reserves to bless others by speaking life. The reservoir in our souls is overflowing with blessings from God, with insight and godly perspective into life’s situations, and with energizing refreshment. We have found life in God to be meaningful, invigorating, and full of purpose, so we are eager and waiting for opportunities to spill over verbal blessings into the lives of others. Speak life!

Cheryl and I often lead seminars on topics matching the need of a group, such as marriage enrichment, spiritual gifts, anger management, setting boundaries, strategic missions thinking, raising boys, servant leadership, house churches, and so forth. The *Lead Like Jesus*[12] seminar is a journey into becoming spiritually minded servants of others. To help those receiving the training develop the habit of speaking life to others, we form a circle of chairs. Half of the participants sit in the chairs. The other half stand behind one of those chairs. Those standing are instructed to whisper into the ear of the person in front of them something they wish they could have heard more often as they were growing up, from a parent or other significant person. Most of the words spoken are affirmations they would like to have heard when they were young, such as “I love you unconditionally,” “You are very smart,” “I accept you just as you are,” or “I am proud of you.” Every now and then someone whispers something like “My child, you’ve been so good. I’m going to give you that red Ford Mustang you’ve been dreaming about!”

Those standing whisper their way around the circle, moving to the person in the chair to their left, and whisper those same words, continuing to do so until they have gone full circle behind the chairs. At that point, those who were seated stand, and those who were standing sit, and the process begins all over again. A final two rounds are then done, this time using scripture verses that speak life to others.

By the time the exercise is complete, everyone has been blessed. Those who spoke life see the effect of their words. Many people begin crying when they are blessed with so many affirming words. others experience an immediate relaxation of tension that had built up in their bodies. A few recognize their own unmet needs and begin a healing process. Some begin to laugh with deep joy. At the end of the exercise, the joy in the room is obvious. People have spoken life to others and have heard words of life.

How can you speak life to others? Think of the words you would like to hear. Begin speaking those words to others. Make a scripture search of verses that can speak life to others. Memorize those verses, and when the moment is right, speak them to others. Here's an example: "Do not fear, for I am with you; do not anxiously look about you, for I am your God. I will strengthen you" (Isaiah 41:10).[13]

Being a verbal blessing to others begins by speaking life, but there is more.

Speak Healing!

Pleasant words are a honeycomb, sweet to the soul and healing to the bones. Proverbs 16:24 (NIV)

Loving, reassuring words, spoken in the face of hopelessness, help heal the soul. Speak kind words that nourish. Pleasant, gracious, generous words help the frazzled mind to unwind. Let your breath blow gentle words that soothe the soul like smooth jazz. Let your words create an oasis of safety, acceptance, and renewal.

Parents, your words to your children are especially powerful. Affirm their character strengths. Help them identify their abilities. Take their dreams, and with a sanctified imagination, verbally paint pictures of your child's future possibilities. Your child may be unsure of your love. Without the spoken word of blessing from the parent, the child may grow up to be less than healthy emotionally. Unhealthy emotions can take a toll on physical health. Parents, regardless of the age of your children, speak healing into their lives. Say to them "I love you. I accept you as you are. You do not have to earn my blessing. You do not ever have to fear my rejection. I will always and unconditionally love you, regardless of what you do or don't do." Does your child, even if he or she is an adult, need to hear those words from you? Speak healing! Then let your words be backed up by your actions.

"The tongue that brings healing is a tree of life" (Proverbs 15:4, NIV). Regardless of whether you are married or single, you have daily opportunities to speak health to others. Sensitive friend, learn to read the hurting hearts of others, and speak health. Is there a friend who has just lost at love? Speak healing into her "achy-breaky heart." Are you in a marriage that has gone sour? Often, one spouse speaking health back into the relationship can bring about restoration. Adult children, refuse to speak cruel words to or about your aging parents or grandparents, but instead speak words that invigorate them with health in their golden years.

Kind words are sweet like honey. Honey has many nutritional elements within it, and it is twice as sweet as sugar. Honey can be substituted into your recipes in place of sugar, and you only need half the amount. Kind words are a vital ingredient in the recipe for living wisely. Eat locally produced honey, and your body may develop better immunities and have fewer allergies. Let your words be locally produced honey, giving health to others. Roman philosopher Lucius Annaeus Seneca said, "Wherever there is a human being, there is an opportunity for kindness." You are passing through this world only once. If there is any kind word that you can speak to a fellow human, speak it now. You won't be passing this way again.[14]

Though bees have stingers, they rarely use them. They are busy each day creating honey. Speak words that promote the health and nourishment of the soul. Speak words of guidance that help people develop habits leading to mental, emotional, relational, and spiritual health. "The lips of the righteous feed many" (Proverbs 10:21 NASV). People are starving for appreciation. We are all hungry for positive compliments. Do your words sting and hurt, or do they bless and feed?

The wisdom coach says the words we speak can affect the health of someone else's bones. How do kind words bring healing to the bones? Mean, cutting words hurt right down to the bone. The bones are the supporting strength for the whole body. When you hear words that bless you, back bones and muscles work together, causing you to stand up straighter, with your head a little higher. Blood flow increases with the emotional lift you receive, and new blood begins to invigorate your bones from the inside out. Your leg bones and feet bones work with your muscles to set your feet dancing with renewed joy! Choose some healing words today.

A group of volunteers began to read books to patients at UAB hospital in Alabama. Soon, many university students were volunteering to read in nursing homes and hospices as well. The elderly who were blessed by these visitors had something to look forward to each day. They waited in anticipation for the next visit. The group of volunteers has become known as "Healing Words."[15] One of the volunteers particularly enjoys reading to children in the hospital.

A six year old boy was recovering from a heart transplant. The student volunteer read to him books like *The Little Engine that Could.* Seeming to forget all about his pain, the boy's face lit up with the turn of every page. His mom was relieved to have someone caring for her son. These volunteers know the value of healing words. Now players from an Alabama baseball team are joining the action and speaking healing words to those in need.

Speak life! Speak healing!

Speak Encouragement!

Worry weighs a person down; an encouraging word cheers a person up. Proverbs 12:25

Our hearts so easily get worn down with anxiety. People are sagging emotionally, sinking into despair. Some have even hit rock bottom. Depression darkens their days. Unkind words or deeds have crushed the spirit. Someone's life is such a challenge that he is pulling out his hair. A negative work environment has frazzled the soul. Life does not come with a guarantee of health and wealth. Most people you meet are stressed about something. Give others a lift with your words! Cheer up others! Speak encouragement! You'll be lifted as well! An encouraging word makes the heart glad.

Like a plant blossoms with sunshine and water, we as humans thrive with positive words. Look for good things about other people and shower them with verbal sunshine. When the sunshiny words hit them, they perk up. They grow. One encouraging word can lift up someone for several days. If you think good about a person, tell him or her. Your words may spur that person to become all that he or she can be. With your words, make the lives of others more enjoyable. Add value to others. Speech habits are deeply ingrained. Changing the way you speak about others and to others will not happen without intentionality.

Does the idea of speaking encouraging words to others seem awkward to you? We find it easy to brag about ourselves. However, purposefully finding and saying something good about others takes some retraining of the tongue. We just don't know what to say. Maybe we're afraid of rejection or laughter. We somehow think that saying good about others takes something good away from us. On the other hand, you might think it's a bit insincere to say nice things if you don't really, really mean them.

None of those reasons are good enough to stop us from becoming encouragers. In fact, they are excuses. Give encouragement a try. Saying good about others stops the cycle of cutting down each other and gives others the freedom to encourage us in return. An encourager is of great value to others. Remember, "Good people enjoy the positive results of their words" (Proverbs 13:2). For starters, just encourage one person once per day. See how it makes you feel. Keep at it for thirty days straight. Once you notice how encouraging others lifts not only *their* mood but *your own* emotions as well, you may find yourself quickly and easily getting into the habit of speaking encouragement.

When I was fifteen, I tried out for the school play. Mr. Garza was a disc jockey from a local radio station, and he came to direct the play. On the day of try-outs, he pulled me aside and said, "Matthew, you have a deep, clear resonating voice that is pleasing to the ear. Would you be interested in being a DJ at the radio station?" I thought he was joking, but he began calling our house and asking when I was coming to the station. Though I was excited at the possibility of being a DJ, I had some self doubt as well. After a few days behind the mic however, I found myself enjoying the work. His encouragement led to a seven year radio career in three states. Thank you, Mr. Garza, for your encouraging words.

At high school graduation, Dr. Dorothy Nell Rogers offered me a Public Speech scholarship at East Texas Baptist University. I accepted her offer. Little did I know that I would be blessed with four years of verbal sunshine under an exceptional mentor, not just in public speech, but in life. Dr. Rogers seemed to live for the purposes of helping me succeed and giving me the skills to do so. She stands tall as one of the finest Christians that I have ever known. Thank you, Dr. Rogers, for the encouraging words you spoke to me. You saw something inside that long-haired rock and roll disc jockey struggling to find himself. With your words, you made it clear that you believed in me. You refused to put up with mediocrity in the words I spoke, or in the life I lived. They just don't make speech professors like you anymore!

I sometimes wonder where I would be now if God had not brought encouragers into my life. What if they had not reached beyond themselves to encourage me? What if I had not been blessed with Cheryl as a wife, giving me and all those around her the daily warmth of her verbal sunshine? What if I had not been born to my mother, who set a goal in life of being cheerleader for me and my sister? I owe many encouragers for whatever good that comes from my life. Their encouragement inspires me to live as an encourager of others.

Speaking words of encouragement to each other is not just a psychological exercise in mutual mood lifting. The encouragement you give to others actually alters the course of their lives, causing them to rise up to their greatest potential. Who are your encouragers? Who are those that stand on the balcony of your life and cheer you on? Have you stopped to thank them? Who needs your encouragement? What could they become with some verbal sunshine to help them grow?

On Sunday at church, find someone you rarely talk with, and encourage that person. On Monday during your lunch break, make an encouraging phone call to a lonely shut-in. Take Tuesday as the day to catch a co-worker doing something right and tell him about it. Send an e-mail encouragement on Wednesday to a friend experiencing difficulty. Set aside Thursdays to bless with words someone who makes a habit of making your life difficult. Wear your favorite blue jeans on Friday as a reminder to encourage a young person who needs you as a mentor in his or her life. Spend Saturday encouraging your family. By the end of the week, you'll be so encouraged yourself that you won't need a day of rest from encouraging others!

Speak life! Speak healing! Speak encouragement!

Speak Wisdom!

Words of true wisdom are as refreshing as a bubbling brook. Proverbs 18:4

If all we do is lift the mood of others, we have only provided a temporary fix. In fact, we may even cause them to become unhealthily dependent on us. Our words must go beyond emotional support to true substance. We must point people toward new perspectives and different life directions. Learn how to verbally guide others. "The godly give good advice" (Proverbs 10:21).

Sometimes the best thing we can do for someone else is to correct his or her thinking. However we tend to shy away from confronting others. We shouldn't. If we give advice wisely, other people will thank us and seek us out for our prudence. "Timely advice is as lovely as golden apples in a silver basket. Valid criticism is as treasured by the one who heeds it as jewelry made from finest gold" (Proverbs 25:11–12). "The words of the wise bring healing" (Proverbs 12:18). According to these scriptures, to speak wisdom we must...

- Be wise and godly. Develop righteous character, from which wise advice flows. "Only the wise can give good advice. Fools cannot do so" (Proverbs 15:7).
- Learn the art of verbal timing. Timely advice is what we're after here. Be ready when the teachable moment arrives, or try to create such a moment.
- Know something valid to say about the situation at hand. Study the context with both the visible and hidden issues.
- Guide people toward needed change. Correct those you mentor when necessary.
- Seek to bring people to wholeness. Any correction must be done from a heart of love, desiring the best for others.

Duane Falk and I have been best friends since third grade. We grew up together, spending much of our free time at Central Baptist Church in Marshall, Texas. We spent more time in the parking lot playing basketball than we did worshipping in the sanctuary. When our Sunday School teacher, Mr. Stott, left the room to take the attendance record to headquarters, we went out the back window and over to the bus stop for a Coke. No one at Central would have *ever* voted either of us as "Most Likely to Become a Missionary."

Though he was older than I was, Duane humbled himself by staying in the freshman university dorm so we could be roommates. Then during his senior year, he moved out, saying that he had found a better roommate. When he introduced me to Kristy, I fully agreed with him. After Duane and Kristy got married, Cheryl and I soon married as well. Within a few years both couples had children. Later we would all load into Duane's old VW van, pile our little kids in as well, and take off on a two week road trip across the Southwest. That was the first of several joint family vacations. Life is good with good friends! Duane and Kristy have served the Lord overseas for twenty years now, in Africa where we went to visit them, and most recently in South Asia.

Duane tells about a time when someone spoke wisdom to him. "I was working on a large church staff and things seemed to be going well. Then another staff member suddenly became angry. He started threatening me and said he would even tarnish my future. I requested mediation from a supervisor but no help was given. I decided that it would be best for the work if I resigned, so I gave one month's notice. But then I was asked to leave the church with all my belongings by the end of that day."

What was Duane's response? He says, "I was devastated. With tears streaming down my face, I packed up all my books and personal items and loaded them into my car. Then

I called an elderly man whom I respected. The voice on the other end of the phone was warm and assuring, saying, 'Do not strike back! When you are hurting, do not strike back. It will not help anyone.' I listened to his words, and didn't talk to anyone about the matter. God worked it out that within a week I was back working at the church, and today that church is one of our strongest prayer supporters."

Duane is naturally aggressive, just like he was as a high school football player. When hit hard, his human response would be to hit back even harder. He says, "The situation could have been completely different if someone had not spoke wisdom into my life at a critical moment. This man didn't just speak words to make me feel better. He spoke wisdom to me, which helped in the situation. His words continue to help me today as I face life's challenges."

Who needs your words of guidance, correction, and direction today? Speak wisdom! Be done with gossip, lies, cut-downs, and running at the mouth. Instead, let your speech build up those who hear, delivering verbal gifts of life, healing, encouragement, and wisdom. Now, let the wisdom coach of Proverbs spike your speaking ability.

ADVANCED COURSE IN SPEECH WITH SPICE

As a public speech major, I cannot help but notice many of Dorothy Nell Roger's speech techniques appearing in the book of Proverbs. Each one of us must speak before others regularly in some role. It may be an informal group of friends just chatting, or you might often be in situations where you use your voice to influence others. Maybe your livelihood depends on your ability to speak well. Here are the ingredients that will help you become a more effective speaker. Follow these principles and experience compounding verbal interest. Work on the details that will take your speaking to the next level. Here's how.

1. **Pay attention to body language.**

Sometimes it doesn't even take words to lift someone up or bring them down. Often, it is the simple difference between a smile and a frown. "A cheerful look brings joy to the heart" (Proverbs 15:30). Look people in the eye. Smile. Minimize distance between you and those to whom you speak. Walk close to where they are, and even go out and walk among them as you speak. Let your face shine with warmth and understanding. Practice good posture. Exude sincerity.

2. **Do your homework in preparing a good presentation.**

"Instruction is appreciated, if it is well presented" (Proverbs 16:21). *How* you say something is nearly as important as *what* you are saying. It makes the difference in whether or not you get your point across. Plan out your ideas and bounce them off a friend. Then rework them as needed. Before you say your main idea, whet their appetite, so they become eager to take in what you have to say.

3. **Choose persuasive words and stories.**

"The words of the wise are persuasive" (Proverbs 16:23). "The godly think before speaking" (Proverbs 15:28). Think of word pictures that will touch the heart. Come up with more stories than you actually need; then choose the most persuasive ones. The language of this generation is imagery. Use images to convey ideas.

4. Anticipate what the opposition will say in response.

"Patience can persuade a prince, and soft speech can crush strong opposition" (Proverbs 25:15). Not all listeners are ready to agree with what you present. Before their feelings of opposition grow, state their case of opposition for them. That gives you credibility and lets them know you have looked at the issue from their point of view. Then explain softly and patiently why your view is still valid. If your point is truly relevant, then it is worth the work involved in persuading others to accept it.

5. Understate Calmly.

"A gentle answer turns away wrath" (Proverbs 15:1). Don't go into verbal combat mode. Your listeners will tune you out. You do not always have to speak at high intensity in order to be heard. The preacher drone voice is so tiring to listen to. A relaxed, natural voice is much more pleasing and persuasive. "A soft tongue breaks the bone" (Proverbs 25:15 NASV). Sincerity, patience, and calmness will turn the tide in your favor, winning over many who might otherwise oppose you.

6. Say something worthwhile.

Don't waste the time of those listening. Think through what is of value to them and say something that speaks to their need. "The lips of the wise spread knowledge" (Proverbs

15: 7, NASV). The word "spread" is that of a farmer blessing an entire community by spreading seed widely. What do you have to spread as a blessing to others? "Good news from far away is like cold water to the thirsty" (Proverbs 25:25). Say something helpful that you are genuinely passionate about: some information needed, a different perspective, a challenging view, or some good news. Get a relevant message and announce it clearly.

7. **Work on timing.**

"It is wonderful to say the right thing at the right time" (Proverbs 15:23).[16] Pay attention to pace and pauses. Give a moment of silence to let anticipation build before and after saying the more important words. Look for feedback from your audience, and pace yourself accordingly. You may end up moving more quickly through some parts than you anticipated, but then find yourself needing to linger in other areas. Have an overflow of material, should feedback tell you to linger a bit more at one point. Get a mental grasp on the flow of your ideas, and go with the flow. Do not depend on a written outline in front of you.

8. **Depend on the Lord to give you the right words.**

"We can gather our thoughts, but the Lord gives the right answer" (Proverbs 16:1). "For the Lord grants wisdom! From His mouth come knowledge and understanding" (Proverbs 2:6). Offer your mouth to the Lord, and He will speak through you! Cultivate a deep walk with God, and you can speak wherever, whenever, from the spiritual overflow that God provides.

9. **Make it fun.**

"The wise person makes learning a joy" (Proverbs 15:2). Be creative and invent ways to get people involved with you. Use visual aids. Make up activities to drive home the point. Give them something crazy to go home and tell their neighbors about! I once used blow-up globes of the world and threw them at random people in the audience, while saying, "The world is in your hands now. What will you do?" What will *you* do to make what you say fun?

10. **Sit down.**

"A truly wise person uses few words" (Proverbs 17:27). Say what you are going to say. Make it move quickly. Then while people are still wanting to hear more, sit down. If they want to hear more, they can invite you back.

11. **Enjoy good results.**

"Those who control their tongue will have a long life" (Proverbs 13:3). "Good people enjoy the positive results of their words" (Proverbs 13:2). This year, Cheryl and I have been invited back to speak in some great places like Singapore, Thailand, and Hawaii. They told their friends in Australia about us, so we go there this year as well. Learning to speak well brings many positive results. To us, the most satisfying results are the changes we see in the lives of people.

Whether it is a simple sentence of blessing to your child, a kind word to a co-worker, or a ten minute presentation representing a million dollar deal before the board of directors, there is great satisfaction in preparing and delivering words that impact positively the lives of others.

In becoming the kind of person able to speak words of life, healing, encouragement, and wisdom to others, God will change you. Hurting people hurt others with their words. However those who have found God's grace and healing through Jesus Christ are changed people. Changed people change people. Speak words of blessing, and enjoy being used by God to change others.

I have left you hanging about how to respond when someone feeds you dog soup. That surely has created some anxiety within you! What did we say to that lady in Korea? We recovered as quickly as possible from our shock, and said, "Thank you for having us in your beautiful home. This is an unusual event that we will always remember." And that it was!

GO GET THE BALL FOR GRANDPA!

Learning from Life

I met little Haeji on the apartment complex playground. The playground was where I took our boys while I got my language school homework done. Haeji was only six, but informally she was my Korean language teacher. What a great little girl! During formal class every morning in downtown Seoul, my professional Korean language teacher gave me several sheets of impossible homework, but every afternoon at the playground, Haeji got my homework done for me in no time at all!

Haeji's mother started coming to our house for my wife's class in how to make chocolate chip cookies. My role was quality control; taste testing for Jesus! Haeji's mother soon introduced me to her husband. During our early days on the mission field in Korea, the need for stress relief drove me to the tennis court. on the court I could work out my stress, make friends with other guys, and have a spiritual impact on their lives. Haeji's father, Mr. Kim, was one such man.

I soon began playing tennis with Mr. Kim. Centuries ago, Korean history had a position in society called *Yangban.* As a young man of status, education, and wealth, a *yangban* walked with a certain strut of dignity. Haeji's father, Mr. Kim, was a true *yangban.* Soon I introduced him to the *Yangban of yangbans,* and after several months of Bible study and sincere discussions, Haeji's father surrendered his life to the Lordship of his Creator. Later, Mr. Kim became the international marketing director of Korea's best ski resort, and has since provided us with many days of free skiing. God is good!

One day on the tennis court, a group of Korean grandfathers asked me why I never played tennis with them. They told me to come out to the court the next morning at six thirty to meet them. As I rubbed the sleep out of my eyes and made my way to the tennis court, I thought to myself, *In a country like Korea, where so much respect is given to the elderly, what's it going to be like to play tennis with grandpas?* Beginning the moment I arrived at the court, my question was adequately answered.

"You there! Listen up. Here's how to play. Rule number one: don't hit the tennis ball where a grandpa is not standing. He can't run fast enough to get to the ball. Rule number two: when you hit the ball straight to the grandpa, don't hit it fast. He won't be able to swing in time to hit a fast ball. Got it?"

Laughter would have been an undignified response, so using the most polite Korean possible, I replied, "Yes sir, oh honorable elder."

"You're young, so you serve first."

I went to the serve line, and tossed the ball up to serve, but before I could swing my racquet, all three grandpas started scolding me. "What do you think you are doing? You don't even know what to do before serving the ball to a grandpa!"

I replied with a bit of sarcasm, "Be gracious to me, oh Grandfather, for I am just an ignorant American who needs to be taught your ways."

"Before serving the ball, you must bow, like this!" He then proceeded to show me a slow, respectful bend of his body from the waist. From then on I bowed to each grandpa each time I served, an exercise which made for an incredible amount of bending at the waist! Little did I know that one symbolic bow at the beginning of the first game was all they expected. Not knowing however, I just kept bowing.

I could put up with all that happened that morning until one of the grandfathers thought he was playing baseball, not tennis. He hit a homerun! The ball went over the fence and across a very busy street. All of the honorable elders, not just the three on the court, but the ten or so grandfathers who had gathered beside the court to amuse themselves at the sight of the ever-bowing foreigner, *all* became quiet and still. None of them said a word or moved toward the gate to get the ball. Together with their eyes, they said to me, "Go get the ball."

As an American, the thing I wanted to say in that moment was, "In America, this is rule number one: he who hits the ball goes to get the ball." However, it didn't seem quite the thing to say. So, I went to get the ball. And again I went to get the ball. And again. And each time, I found myself thinking, *These grandpas are enjoying giving me this torture. They're laughing their heads off watching me being trained to fetch like a dog!*

In the fourth or fifth fetching run, there was nothing left for me to do but pray about my own attitude. It was then that I had a clear impression in my mind of 1 Corinthians 9:22. In allowing me to become a tennis-ball-fetching dog, God was reminding me of the importance of becoming all things to all people, so that by all means I might win some. I was able to return to the tennis court with a fresh perspective and attitude. God wanted me to be moldable. I was way too rigid. I began laughing with the grandpas. I then asked them to help me understand Korean ways. *Immediately* they told me I didn't have to bow every time I served, and next time I should bring more balls, so I wouldn't have to chase the ones they hit far away. Koreans have shown me how to display proper respect for the elderly.

So you wanna be wise? Go get the ball for grandpa. Dance with grandma.

There is one thing that nearly twenty years of life overseas on the mission field has taught me. I've learned it by enrolling in a very expensive school; The University of Hard Knocks. The school has taught me this: God wants me to be a humble, life-long learner.

A learner sees every person as teacher. Haeji was one of my best teachers. One day, Haeji taught me how to count one, two, three; "*hana, tul, set.*" The next day she used the same word for one, "*hana,*" but added the ending "*nim,*" to show great respect for the "One," as she pointed to the sky. That seemed strange to me. Why should a simple number like one have respect given to it like that? I repeated it over and over again. "*Hananim. Hananim.*" Suddenly I had an "aha!" moment. Haeji had just taught me the Korean word for God. He is The One to be respected. From a Korean six year old on the playground, I learned theology!

Every Korean became my language and culture teacher. A learner is someone who does not see himself as knowing it all, but as one who has much to gain from others and from situations. Every tough spot is just an opportunity for God to show me another part of my character that needs refining. A learner is someone who knows that education doesn't equal diplomas on the wall. Learning is having an open mind to see things in a different way, eagerly and daily opening heart and mind to see what changes need to be made in how life is lived. There may be nothing like being dropped down into submersion within a totally different culture to make a learner out of you.

The requirement to be a life-long learner is not just an open mind. It is a humble spirit. We can be open to learning things that will move us up the ladder of success, but which will not make us wiser. A humble spirit makes us willing to learn anything that would make us wiser.

An ancient neglected Eastern book waits to be discovered by you. In it there are hidden treasures. If you find them, they will take you to a different time and place. You will be dropped into the middle of an unfamiliar culture. You will be stretched and challenged to change into a new you. Are you ready for such an adventure? You will discover terse, powerful words written to unleash all of the untapped potential within you. The writer of this ancient text is perhaps the wisest and richest *yangban* who ever lived—Solomon. The book he wrote contains life-giving, ancient sayings from the East. It's simply called "Proverbs." Be warned. If you take seriously the principles found in this ancient text, you simply will not be the same. You will be changed into a life-long learner. You will become a seeker of the rare gem which is the focal point of all the treasures of Solomon: wisdom.

Getting wisdom is the most important thing you can do.
Proverbs 4:7

What is wisdom? Biblical wisdom is not theoretical, but practical. The Old Testament word for wisdom means practical skill for life. The word wisdom is used for artists who built the tabernacle (Exodus 28:3) and craftsmen who constructed Solomon's temple (I Chronicles 22:15). Wisdom is a skillful art. It is the skill of being able to produce long-lasting results in life. Wisdom teaches us how to truly live well, how to build a life that will endure and bless.

Mankind, left to mere intellectual cunning, workplace know-how, and human ambition, may develop an ability to achieve some success without a God-given moral compass or a thought for others. However, don't call that kind of skill "wisdom." Wisdom is a rare God-given ability to handle well the details of life in a way higher than man's way. Wisdom is viewing life as God does, then living by Divine direction. Such a person produces far more in life than a mere high achiever ever could. The exciting thing is that God is not slow to give such supernatural ability. He is eager to give wisdom to all who will receive. By getting wisdom, we are kept in harmony with the principles that God has built into His world. As we discover and live by the original DNA and blueprint for life, things start to work *for* us instead of *against* us.

There are seven words repeated often throughout

Proverbs. These words all attempt to describe wisdom. God promises that those who get wisdom will live securely and will be at ease (1:33). What is wisdom? Here's Solomon's seven-fold answer.

- *Instruction* (Proverbs 1:2) is the leadership of parents in molding a child's habits and character. Following instruction brings length of days and years of life (Proverbs 3:2).
- *Understanding* (Proverbs 1:2) is the ability to pause and learn the true value of an experience.
- *Prudence* (Proverbs 1:4) is being street smart: intuition that sees the reasons behind the way things are.
- *Knowledge* (Proverbs 1:4) describes specialized skill in a particular ability, such as hunting (Genesis 25:27), sailing (II Chronicles 8:18), and playing music (I Samuel 16:16). Knowledge will be pleasant to your soul (Proverbs 2:10).
- *Discretion* (Proverbs 1:4) is to understand a matter thoroughly and then devise a smart plan. Discretion will guard you (Proverbs 2:11).
- *Learning* (Proverbs 1:5) is the idea of getting a grip on something: to wrap your mind and heart around a thing.
- *Counsel* (Proverbs 1:5) is similar to the verb for steering a ship. To receive counsel is to have the ship of your life steered in the right direction.

Together, these words give a summary of what Solomon means by wisdom. Those who allow wisdom to integrate their lives into solid wholeness find the Lord is a strong shield before them (Proverbs 2:7). Getting wisdom may just be the most important thing you can do.

How then do you get wisdom?

1. **Get Wisdom: Fear the Lord.**

Fear of the Lord is the beginning of wisdom.
Proverbs 9:10

What does it mean to fear God anyway? Is fear always a negative thing, or can it sometimes be healthy? You've seen the tee shirts that say "No Fear." Let's play out what life is like without fear. If a person has no fear, then he or she is totally free to do anything. She is free to walk down the middle lane of traffic on the interstate, since she does not fear getting hit by a car. He is free to rob a bank and kill others to gain money, since he does not fear life imprisonment. Is fear always a negative thing? Hardly. Fear can be very good for your health.

Why should we fear *God?* It is because the fear of the Lord is where getting wisdom begins. It's the launch pad for starting out well in life. Fear of the Lord is the headwaters for all the blessings that will flow into the river of your life. Without the headwaters, the riverbed is dry. Fear of the Lord opens a channel for God's truth to flow right into the core of who you become.

We should fear the Lord because of what the alternative lifestyle would do to us. The one who chooses not to fear God becomes a self-sufficient fool, rejecting and even despising solid life principles. His own lifestyle choices bring shame to him.

The wise inherit honor, but fools are put to shame.
Proverbs 3:35

What does it mean to fear God? Robert Jeffress, in his great little book *The Solomon Secrets,* gives three solid answers. First, to fear the Lord means being overwhelmed by God's greatness. The creative handiwork of God is so vast, that our response must be one of awe. Suppose you could climb into a spacecraft and travel at the speed of light–that would be 186,251 miles covered every single second. It would take you 125,000 years just to get across our little Milky Way Galaxy. And ours is just one of millions of galaxies out there. To think that it all came about by chance requires more faith than I have. Sir Frederick Hoyle, a former atheist, became a believer in "intelligent design," and said that the odds of a protein randomly forming and evolving into this earth would be about the same as a tornado whipping through a junkyard and assembling a ready-to-fly Boeing 747 airplane.[17] The awesomeness of creation should cause us to fear God.

To fear God also means to be in awe of God's holiness. He is the King. Our family often retreats to relaxing Thailand, a country of friendly people, cheap accommodations and great food, along with beautiful mountains and beaches. The King of Thailand is given tremendous honor. Before a movie is shown in any theatre in Thailand, every one stands to their feet before a picture of their king. Huge pictures of the king are placed at the entrance of each city. They love their king so much that one day each week, everyone in Thailand wears a yellow shirt to show their love for their king. Many people wear yellow shirts every day. If a Thai person were to actually have the chance to stand before the living king of Thailand, the person's knees would surely knock together in awe of the king.

In his book, Jeffress says "there is a tremendous gulf between a holy God and us-one that we can never bridge by ourselves...A person will never be motivated to receive the forgiveness Christ offers until he develops a healthy fear of God, which comes from a realization of the holiness of God."[18] Be in awe before the King of kings!

A third meaning of fearing God is to re-order our behavior. A new bride fears she might cook a meal that displeases her husband, so she checks with her husband about what he likes to eat, and then works hard to find the needed ingredients. She fears the food might not be ready when he gets home from work, so she gets an early start. Though she's afraid things will not turn out well, her fear is not fright. Her fear is a behavior-alternating desire to serve the one to whom she has given herself completely. To fear God is to live life knowing it is only through Him that we live, move, and have our being. To fear Him is to make pleasing Him the over-riding passion of your life.[19] Give yourself to Him completely.

Let's visit a scene in the early manhood days of the wisdom man—Solomon. This scene occurs as his father, King David, grew old and called his son Solomon to his side for final instructions. Here's what David said to his son.

Take courage and be a man.
Observe the requirements of the Lord your God
and follow all his ways. I Kings 2:2

As a young king, Solomon established his rule by committing himself and his ways to the Lord. There was no strutting around proudly like he knew it all and didn't need help. His genuine humility and dependence on God's leadership soaked all the way down to his thoughts while sleeping.

> The Lord appeared to Solomon in a dream, and God said, "What do you want? Ask, and I will give it to you!"
>
> Solomon replied, "You were wonderfully kind to my father, David, because he was honest and true and faithful to You. And You have continued this great kindness to him today by giving him a son to succeed him. O Lord my God, now You have made me king instead of my father, David, but *I am like a little child who doesn't know his way around.* And here I am Among Your own chosen people, a nation so great they are too numerous to count! Give me an understanding mind so that I can govern Your people well and know the difference between right and wrong. For who by himself is able to govern this great nation of Yours?"
>
> The Lord was pleased with Solomon's reply and was glad that he had asked for wisdom. "...I will give you what you have asked for! I will give you a wise and understanding mind such as no one else has ever had...I

> will also give you what you have not asked for–riches and honor! No other king in all the world will be compared to you for the rest of your life!"
>
> I Kings 3:5–13

Do *you* want wisdom? Put yourself in the Solomon frame of mind. He never saw the kingdom as his own, though it was. He said to God, "These are your people. This is your nation. You have put me in this role. I am yours." He recognized God's ownership over everything. Though he was king of a vast empire, he saw himself as a mere steward for the King of kings. He feared God. He so wanted to do what was right before God. That was all he asked of the Lord.

"Just give me wisdom to do the right thing. On my own, I'm just like a little kid, not even knowing how to get to school. So You must take me by the hand and lead me to learn." Solomon did not ask for riches or health. God was so pleased with Solomon's single desire for wisdom, that God said, "Since you are seeking my Kingdom first, everything else will be added to you as well!"

Fear the Lord and turn away from evil.
It will be healing to your body, And refreshment to your bones. Proverbs 3:7-8 (NASV)

Pray as Solomon did. Using your own words tell the Lord, "God, I am like a child who doesn't know his way around. Here I am in a big world that expects me to act like a responsible adult. Help me more effectively do my job and lead others. I want to know and do what is right, avoiding what is wrong. I can't do it without You. This life I'm living is not my own. All I have, who I am, and what I am doing in life–it's all Yours. This life–it's a God-sized thing! I just can't handle it on my own. I need Your wisdom. That's all I ask."

"What comes from the Lord because it is impossible for humans to manufacture? *Wisdom.* What comes from humans because it is impossible for the Lord to experience? *Worry.* What is it that brings wisdom and dispels worry? *Worship.*"[20]

The most important thing you can do is get wisdom. The fear of the Lord is the starting line of a lifelong marathon called "obtaining wisdom." Hear the blast of the starting gun, and run to obtain the precious gem of wisdom. As you run, notice there is no course laid out before you. There are no lanes on the track to show you where to run. Other runners are running off in many different directions. Remember that you have coaches along the way. You must listen to their voices in order to reach your destination.

2. **Get Wisdom: Listen to Instruction**

Hear, my son, your father's instruction,
and do not forsake your mother's teaching;
Indeed, they are a graceful wreath to your head,
and ornaments about your neck. Proverbs 1:8

Remember, Solomon was known as the wisest man of his day. When did all this wisdom begin for Solomon? How did he obtain such depth of wisdom? "Solomon loved the Lord and followed all the instructions of his father, David" (I Kings 3:3). To understand how Solomon gained wisdom, we must go all the way back to his early childhood. Solomon learned almost everything he needed to know in his father's kindergarten.

As a little boy, Solomon followed his daddy around the house. His father was the king. Solomon watched King David and listened carefully to his father's words. He could feel the humble, broken spirit of his father's heart. Solomon observed his dad's boldness in confronting wild beasts and enemies. His dad had that mystical strength my sons call "old man power." David was rough and strong on the outside, but on the inside he had a soft heart. The boy Solomon sometimes saw his father dancing praise before God. He also saw his father weep, pouring out his inner turmoil before his Creator. Solomon felt deeply that his father, though not perfect, was truly a man who loved God and sought to do the Heavenly Father's will.

Do you want to gain wisdom? Learn from your parents. When I was a little boy, my parents served as missionaries in Indonesia. By the time I was in elementary school, my Father was a minister to students at East Texas Baptist University, and my Mother taught English to international students in our home. Every Thanksgiving and Christmas, we opened our home to international students from all over the world. We sang, read scripture and explained it. We then heard the testimonies of believing students. Many of the students who came had no spiritual life or were still deciding what they would believe. Through my parents, many of these students felt the Heavenly Father's love for the first time and eventually became believers. To ground them in the faith, Mother and Daddy would spend months meeting with them weekly.

My parents taught me much about loving people of all backgrounds. They didn't have to use words to teach me. I saw their example and felt their hearts of genuine concern for the well-being of other people. When I became a single pastor at the age of nineteen, I had already received nineteen years of ministry training. I am truly blessed to be the son of John and Mary Nance. Parents and grandparents have much to teach us. God has given wisdom to your parents. Learn from them. Elders are among us for a reason. Dance with Grandma. Go get the ball for Grandpa.

If your parents are still on this earth, go to them with a teachable spirit. Treasure the limited time you have with them. Ask them to tell you what life has taught them, and listen as they speak. Sometimes young people think that parents just don't get it. The older you get, the wiser your parents become. If you still don't get it, pray that one day you will.

What do you do though if your parents really are not wise? Should you follow the evil advice of ungodly parents? You may have parents who are abusive, dysfunctional tyrants. What then? Find a few mentors. That's good advice even for those with godly parents. You need father figures who have practical wisdom gleaned from years of experience. You need mother types that will teach you from their wisdom. Humble yourself as a child before them. Stop all the busyness of your life and sit at the feet of the sages. In today's youth oriented culture, the wisdom of the elders is seldom sought. Develop a teachable spirit. Accelerate the learning curve of your life by humbly seeking out the wisdom of your parents and other elders. Tap into the tremendous potential of others. Partner with people who have experience you don't have, regardless of their age.

Unfortunately you and I are not always prone to listen. We sometimes have a hearing problem. It's called "selective hearing disorder." Our ears register the words, but our minds filter out the ones that don't line up with our own agenda. Those are the words we pretend that we didn't hear. We change "Father Knows Best" to "I know best!" Our human nature is bent toward stubborn self-reliance. No wonder Solomon continually reminds us to deal with our selective hearing problem; he repeatedly warns us about thinking *we* know best.

Lean not on your own understanding…
Do not be wise in your own eyes.
Proverbs 3:5,7

Our family recently spent three years living in a creative access country. Considering the form of government, there was a surprising level of freedom in lifestyle and thought. Those three years were a fun time of learning, once again, another language and culture. We bought bicycles and rode them everywhere we went each day. Our boys, Joshua and Jonathan, often had their bikes stolen, as did I. For Cheryl, though, I bought a bicycle painted bright pink with the words "Romantic Journey" painted in big English letters on both sides. I'm glad that no one was brave enough to ever attempt to steal our romantic journey! When we heard that seniors Charlie and Ann Pearson were coming to visit us from Texas, we bought for their use an oversize adult tricycle built for an adult driver in the front and one American (or two Asian!) adult passengers in the back bench seat.

I hadn't seen Charlie in years. He still had his long, handle-bar mustache with a big grin sticking out from underneath it. I heard him speak. He still had that deep Texas drawl that stretched two syllable words into three or four. Charlie was a gen-u-ine Texas cowboy, straight from his sprawling North Texas ranch. It felt good to let them love on us and spoil us a bit. Then Cheryl and I took Charlie and Anne to a training event we were leading for new believers.

We were living in a harvest field for God's kingdom. Many people were desperate to know their Creator. We found that if we were obedient in sharing about the Lord, at least one out of every five who heard believed. The goal was for these new believers to share with others, form a new group of worshippers, and be trained to lead their own simple churches. On this particular weekend, we had the training in a hotel room. Hotel rooms make good places to baptize people. For the sake of security, only those being baptized and a few of their seeker friends would come. There is a limit to how many people can crowd around a hotel bathtub! We called these events "swimming parties." Grandpa Charlie and Grandma Anne were going to a swimming party!

When we arrived at the hotel room, we found it full of people. Looking around the room, we realized that some of these faces were new. This made us a bit nervous, so I asked our local friends, "Are all of the people that are here supposed to be here?"

"Yes, everyone here has been invited. Don't worry. There are new people here because we shared our faith with many friends and family, and some of them believed and want to be baptized." We then began training, first with a Biblical lesson on baptism from Matthew 28:18–20 and Romans 6. Cheryl translated into English for Charlie and Anne so they could understand the training. I shared with our local friends the biblical model of evangelism and follow-up; when you lead someone to believe in Jesus, you are to teach them to obey Jesus, and you are to baptize them. Jesus said that believers should share their faith and then baptize those they lead to believe. As a result, there should be many people doing the baptizing. You baptize whomever you lead to faith. Simple enough, right?

Well, not exactly. They had never seen someone baptized. How do you baptize someone? I first had to show them how by baptizing a middle-aged man. However, the biggest barrier to our baptism service that day was not their lack of know-how. It was my *abundance* of know how. Everyone was excited when they saw me baptize someone. They were moved by the symbolism of death to sin, burial, and resurrection to new life with Christ. The room became filled with energy. A young lady then identified herself as the man's daughter, saying she was ready to be baptized next. I was caught up in the moment and forgot all about following my own instructions. Instead of letting those who led others to faith baptize them, I wanted to do all the baptizing myself. Sometimes we are so big, we get in God's way. Then from behind me, I felt the firm hand of a Texas rancher on the shoulder of my baptizing arm. Next came that Texan voice.

"Matthew, you ask that girl who she wants to baptize her."

Ouch! That cut straight to my heart. It was like the voice of God Himself speaking to me, just with a southern drawl! I knew the words I had just heard were true wisdom at a moment when I was leaning on my own understanding, but how should I respond? It was a loud room with lots of people, and they would let me do as I would. I could have pretended I didn't hear that voice and just say to myself, "There goes my selective hearing disorder fouling things up again." What is the one thing God has made clear to me in the last twenty years of life on the mission field? God wants me to be a life-long learner. As a learner who wants to get wisdom, I must listen to instruction. I then turned to Charlie, smiled, and said, "You are right, Charlie."

Turning to the young lady, I asked her "*Ni yao xie gei ni shi xi?*" ("Who do you want to baptize you?")

She replied "*Wo de baba.*" ("I want my daddy to baptize me.") A big bruise suddenly swelled up right there on the top side of my big ego. I had gotten in the way of God's plan, so, I got out of the way. That man baptized both of his daughters, who then baptized many of their friends, and the relational chain of baptisms went on. I stepped back and just let it all happen. I felt free from the burden of being center stage. Most of all, I felt blessed that the work was taking a momentum of its own as the locals took over. How relieved I felt that God, in His goodness, refused to let me think I was wise in my own eyes. He sent Charlie all the way from Texas to stop me before I killed the new movement's momentum.

Within three months, several dozen people believed, were taught to obey Jesus, and were baptized into new house churches formed and led by the local people. I had listened to the wisdom of my elder. God gave me not only wisdom, but he also gave me the promised benefits of Proverbs 1:8–9 - a wreath on the head and ornaments on the neck. The new believers, despite the real possibility of persecution, were training and baptizing their friends. That was the promised victor's crown on my head. The new churches formed were valuable gold chains around my neck.

I had gotten it right. I humbly listened to timely instruction. Thank you, Charlie! Thank you, Lord!

Here's my prayer. I hope it's yours. "God, I want to be forever done with leaning on my own understanding. Your wisdom is so much better. Your way is so much higher. I want to listen for the voice of your instruction. Heal my selective hearing disorder. I don't know best. Father, you know best. Speak to me through anyone You want. I'm all ears."

3. **Get Wisdom: Seek out Advice**

The year is 950 b.c. The form of government is monarchy. The basic enterprise is agriculture. The key players are political leaders, merchants, and sages. Imagine you are there among the people of this ancient world into which we have entered.

The hills of the land are covered with herds of animals being moved to and fro, some of them going to the open air market to our far left. To the right, small groups of people are squatting on the ground around old men giving advice. These are the sages; wise men helping people solve the practical problems of daily life.

The words of the sages are not logical, didactic teachings like those of the Greeks who came after them. These ancient Hebrew sages are speaking intuitive words, full of symbols and word pictures. They are street-smart words for life management. The people are leaning in closely to hear every word of the sage. They are desperate to get wisdom.

In the scene we are painting, there in the background is a beautiful super-structure that outshines all other buildings. That is the temple for worshipping God. Never before has the nation had a temple like that. King Solomon built it.

How peaceful and productive everything is. That is because Solomon built a wall of protection around the city. Then over there is the King's palace. It's so fine that even the Egyptians come over to admire it.[21] The Egyptian Pharaoh was so impressed with Solomon that he presented his own daughter as wife for him.

As we take in this ancient Hebrew world, we notice the

people are all happy and content. Thanks to King Solomon, everybody has plenty to eat and drink. Every family is able to afford a house and garden. The economy is steadily growing. Never before have people enjoyed this level of prosperity.[22]

Suddenly, there is the blow of a horn, and all the sages hurry into the King's court. Hundreds of people stop what they are doing and try to squeeze into the court. This is the time each day when all the sages come to hear King Solomon himself speak. Then we see him. King Solomon walks into his courtyard and begins to speak wisdom to all those who will come and learn. This is the King's introduction.

Let those who are wise listen to these
proverbs and become even wiser.
And let those who understand receive guidance.
Proverbs 1:5

Though his political rule expands into broad territories, it is obvious that Solomon is first and foremost a *spiritual* leader. He spends much of his time every day thinking and praying about wise words to share, and then he speaks them to the people. In our imaginary visit to this ancient land, we notice some people around the King are writing on papyrus parchments. Those are the very ancient scripts that we seek. They contain the choicest proverbial jewels from among Solomon's three thousand sayings. Most of the Proverbs are from Solomon himself, while some of them are sayings collected from other sages.

This scene we have just imagined is what actually occurred daily during Solomon's rule.[23] Solomon spoke each day in parables, using plants, animals, and stereotypical people from everyday life to drive home simple, yet profound principles. His daily teaching sessions were the popular place to be. Rugged individualism wasn't the "in thing." Seeking out advice was in. Solomon not only spoke pre-meditated morsels of advice, but he also listened to common people's disputes, and responded with unusual insight. "The people were awed as they realized the great wisdom God had given him to render decisions with justice" (I Kings 3:28).

Soon, Solomon's proverbs became the recognized curriculum for educating young people and would-be political leaders. Even kings from other nations sent their ambassadors to listen to the wisdom of Solomon.[24]

Solomon catalyzed a wisdom-getting movement. All the sages from far and wide came to hear him. Merchants put down their trades to go get wisdom. Solomon whetted the appetite of the people for God's wisdom. He then fed that appetite through speaking prayerfully prepared proverbs. The common people put high value on memorizing the proverbs taught by their king. They rearranged their lives around God's life-giving principles. The result was an unusual paradise of prosperity. Their strong desire to seek out Solomon's proverbs of wisdom woke the people to life, industry, and wealth.

Who is there today who is actually eager to hear the advice of others, put down his work to go somewhere just listen to silly parables? Get real! We are self-made men. We're done with school! I might be reluctantly willing for someone to give me his opinion, but I'm surely not going to take the initiative by actually asking someone to show me where my life needs a mid-course adjustment! Asking for help means admitting that I don't know what I'm doing! Anyway, who is there that knows better than I do? Why should I pay attention when someone comes to correct me?

Worse yet, why should I *ask* them if I need to be corrected? No way!

It's especially difficult when we know that what we are doing is not good in the eyes of the Lord. It presents a two-fold deterrent to seeking wisdom. First, we do not want others to know what we are doing. Second, we don't want to hear them tell us to stop it or to start doing the right thing. As self-made people, we tend to think we know best, even when we know our actions go against God's will.

Today we are drowning in data, while wisdom is nowhere to be found. We certainly aren't lacking for information today. If we need to know about something, we just search for it online. We have an abundance of research data available to us. People today have much more knowledge about the world than those in Solomon's day. We tend to confuse gaining *knowledge* with gaining *wisdom*. The truth is that these are two very different things. The wise person knows what to do with knowledge. With wisdom, a person receives knowledge, then thinks and acts in a godly way.

Unlike wisdom, knowledge is often self-oriented. We are consumed with consumerism. In our luxury spending and fine dining, we find no meat for the soul. "Our national religion is a kind of evangelical consumerism. We even consume things that aren't really things–we swallow the salt water of information by the gallon, while our throats are parched for the springs of wisdom; we consume violence in computer games and on tabloid TV, while we gorge on a home-delivered pizza."[25] Is consumption for self really the whole point of being human? We often act like it is. We have confused the seeking of information with the seeking of advice. When making decisions, often what we need to seek is *not* more information. We need to seek advice from godly people who know us.

I have met people of the earth who have an intuitive approach to life, gleaned from a collective IQ. Such people have escaped the modern online search for information. Instead, they search deeper. To them, gaining wisdom is seen as essential to survival. Years ago, a group of us traveled from Korea up to extremely remote mountain villages near Myanmar. We prepared what we thought was the bare minimum required gear and put it into our backpacks. By the third day of hiking, our packs got so heavy that we dug a big hole and buried all but one of our packs, knowing we could dig them back up on the way home days later. In the one remaining pack we carried only drinking water for us and Bibles to give the people we met along the way.

After more hiking, we finally arrived at a village of about thirty people. The village had no electricity or running water. There was no school. The people all swarmed around us for over an hour, just staring at our big noses. Eventually the village elder invited us to his house for a meal. We watched as these people, without a store within two days of hiking, used methods unknown to us to prepare fire and food. They worked together and talked together. They had no connection to the outside world. However, they had strong connections with each other, and they were not in a hurry. In fact, their concept of time frustrated us. They seemed to know only of morning, afternoon, evening, and night.

We asked him, “How far to the next village?”

He said, “Go that way in the morning until evening.”

We were on a tight schedule, or so we thought. We had to give it up while among them. There were Bibles in their language. We pulled one out. The village elder was able to read. He sat down outside and all the men of the village came to sit around him. Beginning in Genesis 1:1, he read.

He would read for a while and stop for them to discuss what they were reading. This went on for hours. By Genesis 12, it was already time to eat again. After eating, we turned the Bible to the Gospel of Luke, where the elder read to all the men by firelight until bedtime. Their sincere hunger for the truth moved us to tears. My prayer is that our generation of people in our great land will be more eager to seek the wisdom of God than they are to search online. Wisdom is seeking us out.

Wisdom is viewed in Proverbs as a lady crying out from a busy street corner. She cries out loud, but no one is listening to her.

Listen as wisdom calls out!
Hear as she raises her voice!
She stands at the crossroads.
"I call to you, to all of you!
I am raising my voice to all people.
Listen to me!
I have excellent things to tell you.
Those who search for me will surely find me.
Happy are those who follow my ways.
Whoever finds me finds life."

Proverbs 8:1, 6, 17, 32, 35

Wisdom is advertising on the streets, trying to wake us from our mummy sleep walk through life. She calls for our attention. She gives us a glimpse of her jewels and hopes to share them with us. Wisdom: She longs to be heard.

We should long for wisdom. Wisdom: the survival kit for making it through this dangerous jungle of life. Solomon uses a variety of verbs to describe how we should thirst for wisdom.

Treasure
Tune your ears
Concentrate
Search for like silver
Store in your heart (see Proverbs 2:1, 3:1)

Wisdom is not going to force herself on you. You don't get wisdom without deliberately seeking her. To be wisdom's pupil, you must be eager for her to teach you.

It has been my joy to serve as a professor at seminaries in Korea and Texas. What a privilege to mentor God's servants! My former students live scattered around the world, many serving the Lord in some very difficult circumstances requiring much sacrifice. Before I became a professor, I heard other professors warn me that these days students are not very eager to learn. They told me horror stories about students talking on their cell phones during class, not even opening their notebooks in class, and gazing out the window into never, never land.

To my pleasant surprise, my students were not at all that way. I found Korean students to be especially respectful to me as a foreigner who taught in their language. In Texas as well, I found refreshing groups of students, eager to learn from our cross-cultural experience. Thinking back, I can only remember one student in Korea who cheated on a test and only one person who talked on the cell phone during class. I've taught hundreds of students, and that's a pretty good track record, wouldn't you say?

I have a secret I want you to keep. Do you promise not to tell? Here's my secret method for teaching. When the first student began talking on his phone in class, I squirted his face with a water gun full of Coke. I'm not joking! When the first student was caught cheating, I folded his exam sheet into a paper airplane and flew it out the window. Yes, I really did! The students quickly knew they were to respect me. Second, I created innovative, interactive sessions that made it easy and fun for students to learn. Third, I cultivated within my students a dissatisfaction with their current status quo and a desire to change and to seek out the advice of others. At the beginning of each semester, I gave each student a piece of paper with a large "A" written on it. They got an "A" from day one. All they had to do was the work involved in keeping it.

Want to get wisdom?

- Fear the Lord. His water gun is way more powerful than mine! Let Him guide your path.
- Listen to instruction. Be willing to receive correction from others. open your ears.
- Seek out advice. Take initiative in becoming a life-long learner. Let wisdom penetrate your heart.

Pray with me. "God, I want to seek Your will in all I do. My greatest passion is to please You. Direct my daily path. I fear You. I want to listen openly to instruction and correction. Tune my ears to Your wisdom. I'm listening. Let Your words sink deeply into my heart."

GET ALONG!

Mastering Human Relationships

Laughing together!
Playing together!
Crying together!
Sharing together!
Eating together!

That's the stuff that life is made of! It's what we long for! Few things are worse in life than having something to laugh or cry about, but having to do it alone. Far too often we feel the loneliness expressed by Solomon. "Each heart knows it own bitterness, And no one else can share its joy" (Proverbs 14:10 NIV).

My good friend, John Ariwi from Kenya, tells me about

an ancient African story. The men of the village go off to hunt hippopotamus. Together they prowl the land until one of them finds the big beast. He needs help killing it, so he yells to the other village men. In turn, he is expected to share the hippo meat with them. Occasionally, at the site of the slaughter, a self-centered, arrogant man insists that since he killed the hippo, he gets all the meat himself! Then the other village men quietly turn their backs on him and walk away. If he wants all the meat, he must carry the hippo back to his hut by himself, which is an impossible task!

We were not created to be alone. God wants us to learn how to enjoy real relationships with others. Why is that so difficult for us? A pack of porcupines struggles through a winter night. It is so cold they begin to huddle together. Then those long needles of theirs begin to poke each other. They separate themselves. Finally, the bone rattling cold becomes completely unbearable, so they huddle back together again, putting up with the needling. Humans are just like porcupines. We needle each other, but because we need each other, we dare not neglect each other!

Getting along with other people is one of the most challenging and complicated factors of life. It's also one of life's greatest blessings. If we can master human relationships, our lives will be much richer. Some of us do everything we can to avoid rubbing elbows with others any more than we absolutely have to! Others of us work really hard to make sure everyone else is always happy, but at the end of the day we've given to others without receiving anything in return. Then we ourselves feel cheated and unhappy! Our challenge is to mature to the point where we can consistently maintain quality, mutually beneficial relationships with others. That's what we want. We are all hungry (some of us secretly) for deep, meaningful relationships. No wonder Dale Carnegie's

1937 book, *How to Wins Friends and Influence People,* still continues to sell millions of copies around the world!

Relationships are especially difficult in young American culture, where it is sometimes all about "me." The emphasis on individuality makes us prone to the loneliness that comes with living in isolation. We tend to think Frank Sinatra summed up how we should live when he sang "I Did It My Way." Was he ever wrong! Life is not about doing it our way. Life is about doing it God's way-in relationship with Him and in relationship with others. Everything about the Bible is relational-even in the picture of the Trinity.

We often think our relational problems are due to the other person. Sometimes it may really be true; that other person is simply being difficult! Have you noticed? The more we set out to change other people, the worse our relationship with them becomes! Instead of trying to change others, we must focus instead on what we *can* change: ourselves. We need to work on developing the kind of character qualities within ourselves that will help us relate positively even to the most troubling people. After who we are begins to change, we find the real truth. Many of our relational difficulties are not so much the other person, but how *we respond to* that person.

When it comes to human relationships, God wrote the book! He created us and He knows what it takes for us to get along with each other! The Bible is full of wisdom about what to do and what not to do for a relationally blessed life. The book of Proverbs is a great relationship manual. Wise Solomon gives us the ingredients required for a life full of good human relationships.

Begin treating other people the way you would want to be treated yourself. It's not always the case, but more often than not, other people treat you the same way you treat them. Seek their good. You will find goodwill returning to you.

He who seeks good
finds goodwill.
Proverbs 11:27 (NIV)

The key to good relationships is to seek what is good for other people. Instead of trying to receive benefit from others, seek to benefit others. Quit trying to receive all the love you need. In that mode of living, love will always elude you. Give love to others. You'll generally find plenty of it coming back to you in return. Be a giver not a taker.

How do you seek the good of others? Let's explore five keys to mastering human relationships.

Key Number One: Become an Understanding Person with Whom Others Are Willing to Share Their Heart

---

The purposes of a man's heart are deep waters,
But a man of understanding draws them out.
Proverbs 20:5 (NIV)

People are much like onions. They both smell. They both can make you cry, and they both add flavor, right? Though that may all be true, what I want you to think about here is that they both have multi-layers. Human beings have emotional and psychological layers. It takes a lot of peeling through those layers to really understand what is on the inside of another person. Each of us has his own agendas and purposes, and they are hidden deep within the waters of the soul.

Sometimes we don't even understand the motivations hidden behind our own behavior. We can't get a grip on what's happening inside ourselves until we verbalize it to someone else. That's why God gives us other people. They can see things about us that we can't. They can draw out those hidden, deep waters of our hearts and help us understand ourselves better. We need the help of others in looking at the layers of our lives.

When we are in tune with our deepest inner-selves through the help of others, we are much sounder in our thinking and living. The result is that we have psychological integrity. We are no longer a "fake"–just concerned about the outer layer's image. We become more and more "real" in the inner layers because we have allowed our true inner-self to be known by others. In so doing, we come to know ourselves better. We find acceptance by others who really know us on the inside. That's when life becomes what it was meant to be! Quit spending so much energy on faking other people out! Just be your real self, and if you don't know who that is, let other people help you discover you!

Be who you is,
Cause if you ain't who you is,
Then you is who you ain't!
Harry Hein

I get tired just thinking about that kind of life!

Mental Illness	Mental Health
• starts when we don't let others know who we really are • isolates us from others • results in beliefs not based on reality	• begins when we allow the deep waters of the heart to be revealed to others. • requires a person who has the ability to draw out the deep purposes of your heart. • is possible when you hear and accept what that person reveals to you about yourself. • becomes yours when you respond with willingness to change. • happens through God's power at work, using one person to help another see who they are now, why they are that way, and who they need to become.

Where do we find these people who are able to help us understand ourselves? More often than not, the people that we really need in life are *friends*. Where do we find that kind of true friend? The answer is in the mirror. Become that kind of person yourself! Become someone who is able to draw out the deep waters within the hearts of others.

Ears that hear and eyes that see–
The Lord has made them both.
Proverbs 20:12 (NIV)

How do we draw out the deep waters within the hearts of others? First, become an observer of human nature. God has created us to be observant as we go through life. Sit in the food court of the mall and watch people. He gave you eyes to see the joy of families in the park playing and laughing together. He gave you ears to hear the lonely cry of the one walking solo down a crowded city street with head ducked low. Be in tune with people.

Be observant like Solomon. So many of his Proverbs are simply his observations into how humans behave. He was a sociologist! Here are just a few of his observations about how humans are wired.

- "Hope deferred makes the heart sick, but when dreams come true, there is life and joy" (Proverbs 13:12).
- "Laughter can conceal a heavy heart; when the laughter ends, the grief remains" (Proverbs 14:13).
- "The human spirit can endure a sick body, but who can bear it if the spirit is crushed" (Proverbs 18:14)?
- "As water reflects a face, so a man's heart reflects the man" (Proverbs 28:19 NIV).

This world needs more people like Solomon; people who seek to understand the human heart.

Second, seek understanding into how particular people around you are wired. Draw out the purposes hidden deep within the hearts of a few significant people. Diving into deep waters is dangerous, but it's worth the risk. Dive in! You are not seeking to tear these people apart, criticize them, pretend you have psycho-analytical skills, or tell their fortunes! You are simply trying to get to know them better.

Of course, this requires two things that are difficult. First, we would have to listen rather than talk. Second, we would have to focus on others rather than ourselves. Are you willing to be quiet and tune your heart to the needs of others?

If they have already allowed you to be their friend, you already have their permission to care about what's going on inside of them! However, you must dive into the waters of each heart, swim around with your goggles on, and take a look at what's down there! There may be a small part of them that feels awkward about the relationship going to the next level. However, if they sense that you really care about them, they may crave the insight into their own heart that you can give. Give them space and time to open up and share with you. It will require a commitment to hear them out to the end, without jumping to conclusions about what you think they are saying. Don't have a judgmental attitude of superiority, or else they will never trust you with their hearts.

Third, talk to them about what you see in each heart. First you dive into their hearts. Then you share with them what you see with your under-water, soul-searching goggles. It's amazing what happens when you give people your ear and your heart. You let them share themselves with you. They pour it all out. Then you share back with them what you have heard them say, and what you see as another perspective on their situation. A light bulb turns on in their head! They understand themselves in a new light! They become free to step over something that was tripping them up. They boldly do what they never dared do before. They become clearer in who they are, and what God's purpose is for their lives.

In 1991, after a year of Korean language study, Pastor Yoo asked me to preach my first sermon in Korean. I prepared for several weeks, and had it all written out. It was a very accurate and thorough treatment of a great biblical text. However, when I was done delivering the message before the people of Holy Light Baptist Church of Seoul, I had no doubt that the message had fallen completely flat. What eluded me was *why* it was not well received. Though the Koreans kindly endured my message to the end, they did not seem to be moved by it. In fact, they were restless with having to sit through all that I put them through. I had pastored for eight years prior to arriving in Korea. God had always blessed, inspired, and challenged people through the words He gave me to share. Unfortunately it just didn't happen that day at Holy Light Church of Seoul. Were my preaching days over because I became a missionary? Though I didn't say anything to Pastor Yoo, I went home from church that day very frustrated and confused.

A few days later, Pastor Yoo took me out for a meal. He asked me how I felt about my preaching the past Sunday. He listened carefully as I shared my heart with him. It was clear to me that he really cared about what I was saying, and that, despite how I had delivered a sub-par message to his congregation the past Sunday, he accepted me as an equal in ministry.

He said "Brother Na (my Korean name), I want to be

a true Korean brother who looks at you as a peer, not as an American who can bring me money and prestige. It seems like you are tired from adjusting to a new culture and learning the Korean language. You have many Koreans around you all day every day, but you don't have many real friends. I want to be your friend."

Pastor Yoo had seen the deep need of my heart when I had not even verbalized or fully realized what I needed. He was extending to me the gift of friendship. That day I went home feeling like I was truly blessed. Pastor Yoo was my friend!

There was even more! "Would you like to bless people through preaching in Korean just like you have moved people in the States?" Pastor Yoo asked me.

"Yes, of course!"

"In the U.S., people may like hearing a deep exegesis of scripture during the sermon, as if they were at Bible College. However you will never be able to do that well in Korean. Koreans are moved by one simple truth from scripture, looked at from different angles, with each angle having an interesting story that they can remember. Try that next time, and don't use formal, written Korean language. Just talk to us next time."

"You mean you are willing for there to be a next time?"

"Of course I am willing. How about preaching once a month?"

My brother Yoo had become for me a person of understanding, with whom I felt free to share the things of my heart. He had taken the time to care about me and become a true friend, searching the deep waters of my heart. He believed in me and gave me another chance. May you and I become that kind of person for others.

Oh, the comfort–the inexpressible comfort
of feeling safe with a person,
Having neither to weigh thoughts,
Nor measure words–
but pouring them all right out–just as they are–
Chaff and grain together–
Certain that a faithful hand will take and sift
them–
Keeping what is worth keeping–
And with the breath of kindness
Blow the rest away[26]

How can you develop the best relationships possible? First, become a safe person of understanding, with whom many others feel free to share the things of the heart. Then there's a second step.

Key Number Two: Sharpen Each Other

As iron sharpens iron,
so one man sharpens another.
Proverbs 27:17 (NIV)

To sharpen a knife, it takes something tougher than the metal of the knife itself. Cloth or wood just won't sharpen a knife. A soft metal like copper won't either. It takes a file, a piece of flint, or a grinding wheel. In the same manner, we need people to be a bit tough on us to sharpen us. Once a knife is sharp, it is ready for more productive service. However, over time it becomes dulled and needs sharpening again. A dull knife just tears things up and is dangerous. The difficult part of sharpening is that in order to make the knife sharper, part of the knife has to be removed. Seldom do you and I need more things put *into* our lives. We need people in our lives to help us *remove* unnecessary things, so that you and I will be sharper.

Loners have no one to sharpen them. They are like a dull knife, dangerously tearing into things. Here is God's relational plan: one person sharpening another person. The original language says one man is to sharpen *the face* of another. The word face in the Bible is used of a person's actual appearance (Proverbs 25:23; I Sam. 16:7,12; Dan. 1:13–15; Matt. 6:16), the expression of feeling toward another person (Proverbs 16:15; Gen. 31:2; Ps. 4:6; 44:3; Acts 2:28), and the spirit, demeanor, behavior, or conduct of a person (Proverbs 15:13; Deut. 28:50; Ps. 10:4; Eccl. 7:3; Dan. 5:6,9). Real relationships involve sharpening another person's countenance, ability to express feelings to others, and behavior.

Character is created in community. Sharpening others sometimes means encouraging. At other times, it means challenging. Sometimes it means re-directing. Other times it means partnering. However, it never means ignoring. Iron sharpening iron means being engaged in each other's lives. The result of sharpening is a person who is more fit for useful service-a person who, due to the sharpening received from friends, is more productive and happy in life.

Some of the neatest things happen in life when you bounce ideas off a good friend. The friend carefully listens to your idea, gives you some suggestions for how it might need tweaking, or gives you a similar but altogether different idea. You and the friend may form a partnership to pursue the dream you created together. The strength gained from two people doing something together is quite remarkable. Before you know it, something incredible is happening that would have been impossible if you had not let iron sharpen iron. Both of your lives are being changed for the better.

Have you ever had an accountability partner or group where you shared honestly with each other about your lives? You gave permission to question each other on specific moral or personal issues. Sometimes, such close encounters of the heart can really be scary. If, however, you've ever once experienced the life changing value of honest, open relationships on matters deep in the heart, you know about iron sharpening iron.

Do you know what's sad about most of us? For whatever reason, we sit around trying to sharpen our own iron. We're afraid of contact with other iron. It will hurt. Sparks will fly. Parts of who we are will fly away, never to be seen again. We will change, and that just won't do. How long has it been since you asked a friend his advice on a decision you are considering? How long has it been since you took the risk of dreaming out loud together with a friend? That's how long it's been since you've been sharpened. We need sharpening regularly, or life grows very dull. A knife cannot sharpen itself, and neither can a life.

This past week I spent all week in intensive training activities with believers in a creative access country. When they decided that each day would be started at 6:30 with "Quiet Time," I pictured in my mind people scattered around the room here and there, each in their own little private space quietly meditating on God's Word. That's how Americans would have done it. However at 6:30 the next morning, they all bent their knees together in a circle, announced the text they would all look at, and spent an hour looking at the passage. It was usually quiet, but occasionally someone would share what God was convicting him about from the passage. Then it would be quiet again. After a while, someone would respond with how God had challenged him through what his friend had shared. This group quiet time experience had much intensity and meaning, because when someone shared, God used it to move someone else in the group to realize an area where he needed personal change. It was iron seriously sharpening iron.

American rugged individualism has crept into our lives so deeply that we feel there is greater value to the lone-ranger approach to life. You won't find group synergy in the old, tradition-prone boulevards of historical America. There you only find the rugged, pioneer spirit that made us into such strong-willed, stubborn individuals.

Fortunately there *are* places and times when modern Americans are especially good at bonding together and using relational energy to do what seems impossible. You find it in the tech labs, the think-tanks, sometimes even the e-chat rooms, and on the higher-output end of society where Americans know they really need each other to get the job done.

Our space program is a fine example. Many years ago, our younger son Jonathan and I flew to NASA in Florida to attend Space Camp. Together with other dads and sons from around the country, we went through space travel preparation training. They tortured me by putting me in that machine that whirls you around at one hundred times the force of gravity. All right, maybe it was only three G's, but it took my body at least three days to unscramble itself after that!

On the last day of Space Camp, we did what we had been training to do. As a team, we went into the flight simulator and sought to complete the mission we had been given. It took high level teamwork to make sure all the tasks were done. While we were sweating it out together, the NASA instructors were looking on from outside the space module.

Then they threw us a curve ball. By creating some problems for us that were not at all planned, the NASA team tested our response to stress and our ability to function as a team, even under crisis. We had to quickly respond to the crisis and together determine what needed to be done. We each had to set aside personal tasks and focus on one thing: what we needed to do to accomplish the mission. Even though it was just simulated flight, it didn't feel like it at the time! I have good news! We made it back to earth without crashing! I'll never forget: NASA is well aware that iron sharpens iron.

How can you master human relationships?

Become someone with whom others feel the freedom to share the deepest things of the heart. Be an observer of human nature. Explore the hearts of those closest to you. Tell them what you see going on in each heart. Do so because you genuinely care, not because you are judging them.

In your relationships with others, let it be iron sharpening iron. Ask those close to you to challenge and sharpen you. Be open to hear what others are saying and be willing to respond with personal change. Tell them you need their help so that you can see lasting change in your life. Changed people change people. God wants you to master human relationships. Here's another key to mastering human relationships.

Key Number Three: Recognize and Honor Relational Boundaries

Do not move an ancient boundary stone
set up by your forefathers.
Proverbs 22:8 (NIV)

In Solomon's days, real estate dealings were marked by forefathers who placed stones on the corners of the family property. It would be possible to move the stone just prior to a real estate exchange, capturing more than your fair share of the property. If Grandpa were no longer around, what would it hurt to move it just a little? People who live as takers sneak around moving boundary stones to their advantage. Sometimes those boundary stones are actual ones. Sometimes they are relational boundaries.

During our first pastorate in the United States, a neighbor of the church insisted that the driveways into the church parking lot were actually on his property. He wanted to sell us that portion of land for several thousand dollars! We hoped to maintain good relationships with him, yet at the same time not let him take advantage of us. So we offered to build an attractive fence at our expense, after a county surveyor visited to re-establish the boundary. We thanked the neighbor for showing us the need to make the boundary sure. He knew from our nice but firm approach that we would be neighborly, but not dumb.

Set boundaries. Doing so shows others that you are a person of integrity, looking for a mutually beneficial relationship, not a lop-sided one. Word will get out that you can be trusted to deal fairly with others and that you expect the same in return.

Recognize both geographical and psychological borders. Togetherness is great. However, each of us needs his own space and time. Don't be afraid to tell others when they have approached your limit. Likewise, if you have stepped over someone else's boundary, step back.

We often think good relationships have no limits, but the opposite is true. The best relationships are those when people clearly define together what is in bounds and what is out of bounds.

Could you imagine the Super Bowl being played without definite field boundaries? If you want to thrive at human relationships, enjoying them to the fullest, establish and honor clear boundaries.

Our relationship with God is of the highest priority to Him. He also wants people to have great relationships with each other. That's why he established definite boundaries for our spiritual forefathers; these are known as the Ten Commandments. They are valid fences for today, providing relational freedom. Boundaries give us the power to say no. The results are true freedom of the soul and lasting relationships.

There are times when you must say, "You have offended me." At other times you must say, "I have wronged you. I am sorry." "We should not be doing this. It's wrong." "I do not agree with you." "Let's not go there." "Tell me why you are irritated with me." "I'm tired of this." "You've gone too far." "Let's DTR: define this relationship." Boundaries assure fairness. With boundaries, the relationship is truly mutually beneficial.

Boundaries help us to avoid living as takers. Don't move the ancient stones handed to us by our spiritual forefathers. The fifth commandment on those stones helps us to avoid living as takers in relation to our parents. The sixth reminds us not to take someone else's life. The seventh tells us not to take another person's spouse. The eighth helps us not to take someone's possessions. The ninth commands us not to take another's reputation. The tenth commandment tells us not to even desire what is our neighbor's. Don't be a taker who tries to move boundary stones for personal advantage.

Become someone who is known for fairness and certainty on relational boundaries.[27]

How do you master human relationships?

Key Number Four: Be Loyal Through Thick and Thin

A friend loves at all times,
and a brother is born for adversity.
Proverbs 17:17 (NIV)

The word "love" in the verses refers to a steadfast direction of your will toward the good of another. In a word, it's "loyalty." That describes God's relationship to us. He is consistently directing himself toward our long-term good. Does that describe how you relate to others? Are you someone who is looking out for the good of others? What changes need to take place in how you relate to others?

The verse is not about finding a loyal friend. It's about becoming one. Fair weather friends walk out when you mess up your life. Foul weather friends walk in when others are walking out. Become a loyal friend who is there at all times, through thick and thin. A brother, whether by actual blood or by the bond of brotherly friendship, exists for the purpose of giving support during life's toughest times. Be like a loyal blood brother to your friends.

That will require maturity. It will require you to be committed to work it out, whatever it takes. I pray that you and I are blessed with those kinds of true friends. May God make each of us that kind of friend to others.

Cheryl and I recently watched a hilarious Australian movie called "The Nugget." Three mates find a huge gold nugget out on their fishing land. They decide to split the value of the nugget three ways. However, one mate has a wife who insists that since the fishing land deed is actually in their name only, the gold all belongs to them. She convinces her husband to tell his mates, and the friendships of the three couples are ruined. Finally, he tells his wife that he doesn't care so much about what is legally theirs. He wants to do the right thing by being loyal to his mates.

True mates are those you can lean on through it all.

> Lean on me, when you're not strong,
> and I'll be your friend. I'll help you carry on,
> for it won't be long 'til I'm gonna need
> somebody to lean on.[28]

We each need friends and brothers who will remain faithful to us, even when our lives are a mess. We all wish we had that kind of friend to lean on. When we are lonely and cut off from others, instead of looking for that kind of friend, we must seek to *become* that friend. Who is it that needs you as a true, loyal friend? Go to that person and sing "Lean on Me" with him!

There is another thing we must do.

Key Number Five: Tell It Like It Is: Shoot Straight with Each Other.

Perfume and incense bring joy to the heart,
and the pleasantness of one's friends springs from his
earnest counsel. Proverbs 27:9 (NIV)

Perfume and incense were used regularly for festive occasions, for times of joyful celebration. The kingdom of

God is meant to be a party! The party begins when we shoot straight with each other. The path to partying is earnest counsel. A friend who tells it like it is, giving honest advice, is just as pleasing as a party.

Christians should be masters at relationships. We have real life given to us by God, and we have a family of other believers. Why is it that we are not able to let down our guard with each other? I spoke with several new believers recently who said that before they became Christians, they enjoyed "gut-honest" talks with other guys down at the pub in Wan Chai on Hong Kong Island. They said they used to sit around, tell stories, laugh, and be real. Then came the clincher. They asked, "Why can't we find real relationships like that with Christians?"

We have become masters of hypocrisy. We work hard at portraying the image others expect of a Christian. It certainly wouldn't do to go to church and admit your own moral shortcomings or doubts about God! We must wear our mask of perfection.

In many ways, life in the body of Christ should be more like what happens at a bar. There, people are freed-up to share openly. In a church, the agent that frees us to have vulnerable, honest relationships is not spirits in a bottle, but the Spirit of God Himself among and within His body. I applaud the new wave of simple churches springing up around the States: new churches that seek to recapture the informal, community sharing and body life of the New Testament house church. Though God is pleased with hundreds worshiping together formally in a beautiful sanctuary, He also knows that we must have *genuine* sharing of ourselves with a few other people. That cannot happen in a structured, formal worship service. We need to gather in small groups to pour out all of our joys and struggles.

In these small groups, we find mutual caring and honest rebuke.

Where is the verse in the Bible that commands Christians to take ourselves so seriously? The longer we follow Christ, the more we seek out gloomy, narrow-minded believers, exactly like ourselves! Good grief! We look like we need someone to come tickle us, and help us to loosen up a bit! We are not enjoying friendship with others the way God wants us to! Life is meant to be enjoyed! People are placed in our lives to be pleasant and festive. People of God, let's party! Let's take our masks off and share our real selves with each other.

Our ability to party with believing friends is in direct proportion to our honest, open vulnerability to give and receive straight advice. Giving advice involves the risk of offending a friend but brings the reward of a deeper relationship. Learn to give advice in a way that will be well received. Receiving advice or rebuke means having a humble, teachable spirit and willingness to change. "An open rebuke is better than hidden love! Wounds from a friend are better than many kisses from an enemy" (Proverbs 27:5–6). "He who rebukes a man will in the end gain more favor than he who has a flattering tongue" (Proverbs 28:23 NIV).

Don't think of a rebuker as an enemy. He may very well be your best friend. Those who are willing to rebuke you are your true friends. The pain you feel from their correction simply means they care about what's best for you. Learn to find the kernel of truth in the criticism, change your ways, then thank the critic! Trust the critic to be honest with you.

Those "friends" who keep kissing up to you, and only flattering you with praise, may actually be your enemies! Your neighbor doesn't want flattery from you. It makes him feel like you may be setting some kind of emotional trap for him. "Whoever flatters his neighbor is spreading a net for his feet" (Proverbs 29:5, NIV).

Two weeks after we were married, Cheryl and I moved near Houston, Texas to start a new church. For a while, worship for our new believers meant moving folding chairs before and after worship. I put one of the new believers, a senior adult named Drew Waldrop, in charge of chair duty. Every Sunday night as he was working with other men putting up the last of the chairs, I would come to him and say "Thank you, Drew." I never got a positive response from him, which puzzled me. One Sunday night after hearing my thank you, he said "Matthew, do you really think I'm doing this for you?"

It caught me off guard at first, but now I can say I don't know that I have ever had a better rebuke. In that moment I quietly thought about what he had said, then eventually responded. "Drew, you are right. I have been looking at ministry as trying to get people to serve me. It's not about me. I'm glad you're serving Someone way more important than me. I promise I will try hard to never thank you again!"[29]

Starting the next Sunday night, I developed a new habit. I came up to Drew as he finished folding the last chairs, held my open hand up high in the air, and said "Let's do a high five for another fun day of serving God together!" Drew would grin real big and slap my hand with an enthusiastic high five! That's the party that results from earnest counsel.

How many really reliable friends do you have– friends that will stick with you through thick or thin? They accept you not because of how near perfection you are. They simply accept you as you. A true, loyal friend is very rare in this life. A true friend walks in when others walk out on you.

Many a man claims to have unfailing love,
but a faithful man who can find?
Proverbs 20:6 (NIV)

Out of the furnaces of war come many true stories of sacrificial friendship. One such story tells of two inseparable friends during World War I. They had enlisted together, trained together, were shipped overseas together, and fought side-by-side in the trenches. During an attack, one of the men was critically wounded in a field filled with barbed wire obstacles, and he was unable to crawl back to his foxhole. The entire area was under a withering enemy crossfire, and it was suicidal to try to reach him. Even so, his friend decided to try. Before he could get out of his own trench, his sergeant yanked him back inside and ordered him not to go. "It's too late. You can't do him any good, and you'll only get yourself killed."

A few minutes later, the officer turned his back, and instantly the man had gone after his friend. A few minutes later, he staggered back, mortally wounded, with his friend, now dead, in his arms. The sergeant was both angry and deeply moved. "What a waste," he blurted out. "He's dead and you're dying. It just wasn't worth it."

With almost his last breath, the dying man replied, "Oh, yes, it was, Sarge. When I got to him, the only thing he said was, 'I knew you'd come, Jim!'"

One of the true marks of a friend is that he is there when there is every reason for him not to be, when to be there is sacrificially costly.[30]

Except for your relationship with God, there's nothing

more important on this earth than your relationship with other people.

Set this as a high priority in life; that when you die, you will have developed deep, meaningful relationships with key people God has placed in your life.

Jay Kesler states it well when he says

> "One of my goals in life
> is to wind up with eight men
> who are willing to carry one of my handles."[31]

LIVING AT PEACE WITH THE SEXUAL PART OF SELF

How to Be Pure without Moving into a Monastery

Shortly after winning the 1986 Super Bowl, Mike Singletary became afraid of the dark. This is no joke: He slept with a light on. Fear, in fact, overwhelmed his life. We're talking about Mike Singletary, the Chicago Bear who was named to nine Pro Bowls and earned the nickname Samurai. Night after night he could not sleep unless the light was on. What he feared was himself. He wasn't sure who he had become. Mike had no peace within.

There was Mike Singletary, the Christian. He was saying the right stuff. Mike was a star athlete, and supposedly near to God, but it was all just shiny, bright lies.

Then there was Mike Singletary, the man in the mirror.

He knew he was a fake who could not be trusted. He didn't even trust himself. His sin began with the pride of believing that his accomplishments were his own. He was damaging himself by living life on his own terms.

Mike's root problem was pride. This pride led to self destructive indulgency. During their engagement, he had been unfaithful to his wife. The guilt was nearly eating him alive. However, he knew that was not the worst of it. He had betrayed his God. "I wanted to be a Christian on my own terms," Singletary says. "Everything had to go my own way because I deserved it. That's how I thought."[32]

Do you desire to do what is right with your sexuality? Good for you. It will not be easy, but with God's help, it is possible to live a life of sexual purity even without moving into a monastery. Proverbs gives men and women straightforward help in staying sexually pure.

Warning: some of what you read here may seem drastic. When it comes to sexuality, the pull of temptation is so strong in the wrong direction that the forces pulling you back in the right direction must be even stronger. Be ready for demands to be made of you. Don't discard them just because they seem a bit extreme. As you read, be honest with yourself about how you need to change. Take a serious look at your habits, including mental ones. We'll think first of the male side of the equation, and then the female.

Today, I have just returned home to Hong Kong from a twelve day meeting in Thailand. The Thai are such friendly, gracious people. Nevertheless, Thailand may just be the sex sin capitol of the world. Bangkok is known world-wide for its prostitution industry. Another nearby Thai city is known as the transvestite capitol of the world.

A few of us rented bicycles while we were in Northern Thailand. One day during a break in the meeting schedule, a co-worker named Randy and I took off on our bikes. We pedaled out of town, taking in the fantastic scenery and fresh air.

By five thirty, when it was still an hour from dusk, we turned the bikes back in. Supper would be served at six o'clock, so we began speed walking back to our meeting place. Our legs were still moving at cycling speed. We were hungry, and that motivated us as well. We rounded a corner where a building blocked our view of what would be ahead. Suddenly, standing out in the road blocking our path were about twenty hookers, all competing to gain our business. We were walking so fast we didn't have time to slow down, and the shock of it all caused our reflexes to be slow. Randy and I both panicked as we found ourselves on a collision course with a bunch of prostitutes, and who knows what tourist's cameras would be clicking away to send pictures back to our supporters? Fortunately, the girls saw our speed of movement, and jumped out of our way very rapidly. It was an uncomfortably close encounter of the wrong kind. We sped up to get out of there quickly.

You can begin to understand why, among missionary men, Proverbs is one of the most read books of the Bible. We must do much traveling, often alone. We are as human as other men, and not beyond being tempted. Temptations come along here and there, sometimes in unexpected ways and unplanned places. Maybe one reason why missionary men regularly read Proverbs is for the stern warning it gives repeatedly about sexual immorality. When you pray for missionaries, and for other Christians as well, pray that God will help us live out the purity principles we study in Proverbs. Not a few missionary men have left the field due to sexuality issues.

The principles of Proverbs are not just for missionaries.

They are for all men and women of today's world. The people of today's world have become highly mobile. You may find yourself traveling alone for business purposes. You need God's wisdom to guide you and protect you. Follow the wisdom of Proverbs, and you will be able to live at peace with the sexual part of self.

HOW TO STAY SEXUALLY PURE AS A MAN

Proverbs gives us guys some practical handles on how men should avoid sexual temptation. Ladies, your turn is coming, but for now let's look at the issue from the masculine viewpoint. Though this section of the chapter is written to men, it can also help you ladies understand men better. Guys, here's what Proverbs says to do when faced with sexual temptation.

Ask, "What if my sister were here?"

Say to wisdom you are my sister. Proverbs 7:4 (NASB)

Love wisdom like a sister;
make insight a beloved member of your family.
Let them hold you back from an affair.
Proverbs 7:4–5

Let's pretend you are in a particularly compromising situation. You tell yourself it's potentially just a small compromise, and you are a long way from anyone that knows you. You look around. No one is watching you. What is to keep you from making a wrong choice? If you are like many men, there is nothing that keeps you from doing what feels exciting, daring, and fulfilling. But then after it's all said and done, you have to sleep with the light on because you are afraid of yourself. There is a better way. In that situation, ask "Would I do that if my sister were watching?"

My older sister Elizabeth is always two years ahead of me. I just never can catch up. Growing up, I was always trying to understand the things in her bigger, more mature world. She had so much more understanding than I had. E'beth knew the important role she played in guiding me. I knew that when it came to some of the really important things in a boy's life, like knowing just what approach would result in Daddy stopping to get ice cream (it never took much!), coming up with good names for our cats and dogs, and learning how to speak pig Latin, my sister was someone I could turn to. I should have done so more often. That's the way with older sisters. We can all learn from them if we will.

One reason men do dumb things is we think no one is watching. Don't go alone. Take your big sister, Wisdom, with you wherever you go. Say, "Come on, Sis. Let's go." Then if you find yourself about to compromise, turn to your sister and ask her what you should do. She will stop you from being a fool. Because of the deceiving exhilaration that sexual impurity provides, Wisdom's warnings are strong and blunt. She shouts, "Don't be a fool!" Desperate times call for desperate measures. When you are led by lust instead of Wisdom, your sister will give you a piece of her mind. Listen to her more often. Listen to Wisdom, always.

See the Mystery Woman for What She Really is.

The temptress may appear to be a perfect "ten." On the outside you see only her beauty. You notice her mouth is smoother than oil (Proverbs 5:2), but Proverbs describes her true condition with words such as...

---

immoral...adulterous...abandoned (Proverbs 2:16-17)
...bitter as poison...sharp as a double edge sword
(Proverbs 5:4)
...deep pit...treacherous robber. (Proverbs 23:27)

She has a strategy that is tuned into the deep insecurities of males. She knows how to scratch right where you itch. She is targeting your loneliness, boredom, lust, pride, and insecurity. Put those heart issues out on the surgery table and let the Master surgeon circumcise your heart.

Guys, would you eat meat set before you if you didn't know what animal it came from? Why go outside the home to eat used, recycled, canned mystery meat when you can feast on the steak of your own spouse? You already have the best in your own bed.

Once there was an Indian chief who was led to Christ by a missionary. A few days later, the missionary returned to the chief to ask how he was doing in his spiritual life. The chief sat cross-legged for a moment, in deep contemplation, then spoke. "Two dogs fight inside me."

Perplexed, the missionary did not know how to respond. To keep the chief talking, he asked the chief "Which dog is winning?"

"The one I feed the most."

For each person who would live holy, there is spiritual

warfare in the soul, between the flesh and the spirit. Starve your flesh. Get rid of all the lustful videos, pictures, songs, friends, magazines, posters, computer files, web sites, and playthings in your life. These things don't give you the full picture. They only deceive and frustrate you. If you are in an inappropriate relationship, break it off. Change your phone number if you have to. Get out before it is too late. Your goal should be to live at peace with the sexual part of yourself. The only way to do that is by living in purity. A pure lifestyle gives confidence and joy.

Feed your spirit. Be filled with the wisdom of God. Your sister wants to meet with you regularly to coach you in how to treat women with respect. She will help you not treat them like sex objects. Get into the word of God. There you will find a treasure chest of wisdom and truth that will re-arrange your life. Fellowship often with other believers. Pray to God and listen to his voice.

A tempter's ways are slippery. She will try to keep you away from serious thought. Nothing feeds sexual impurity like fantasy. Inside your dream world, you drift far away from reality into a make-believe land where you are the king. Wisdom, your sister, will jolt you out of your fantasy world and back to your senses. Inside of you there will be a tug of war between two females–the temptress and Wisdom. Get on Wisdom's end of the rope and pull with her. Victory will be yours.

Look at the End Result, Not the Image Before your Eyes.

Entering her house leads to death; it is the road to hell.
The man who visits her is doomed.
He will never reach the paths of life.
Proverbs 2:18-19

Here is a sobering thought. Solomon, who wrote all these words of wisdom, may have followed them for a season, but then he himself ignored his own advice. Though he had a good start, he didn't finish well. The closing years of Solomon's career are very disappointing. He slid into polygamy. First Kings 11:1–8 tells us that Solomon loved many foreign women who worshipped man-made gods. He had seven hundred wives, princesses, and three hundred concubines. His wives turned his heart away from the Lord. Next he began to build houses of worship to these other gods, and the Lord's wrath was poured out on Solomon. He died an old pervert, worn out from self-indulgence.

If you continue your current sexual habits, what kind of man will you become when you are old? After you die, how will you be remembered? What secrets are you keeping? Those who really know you, intuitively know your secrets as well. What will they tell others about you at your funeral?

How would you *rather* be remembered? What kind of person do you really want to become? Begin living today as if you were that man already. Visualize the kind of man you want to become. One day at a time, with God's power, live like that person. Don't buy into the deceptive ideas that people can't change or that the way you are is just a function of the unchangeable personality you were born with. People, with God's help, *can* change. Get the resources that you need to change. Find people who can help you. You'll be glad you lived with the end of life in view, not just the passing pleasure of the moment.

There's one other form of self-deception that men are good at. You may be saying, "I'm a victim of circumstances. I just happened to be in the wrong place at the wrong time, and the wrong woman just made me do the wrong thing. It wasn't my fault." Real men take ownership for their actions and their thought life.

Two paths are before you. There is the path of sexual purity. It leads to victory and life. There is also the path of lustful pleasure seeking. It looks like a better path, yet in the end illicit sex leads to self-destruction and death. What path will you choose?

Stay with the Group of Guys: Don't Wander Off To a Place of Temptation Alone.

Solomon was an observer of people. If he were alive today, you could probably find him at the international airport sitting and watching people. He learned much about human nature. His people-watching habit influenced greatly the Proverbs that he wrote. The scene we now examine is one that Solomon saw while observing people through his window.

One day Solomon saw a young man "among the youths" (Proverbs 7:7, NASV). Unfortunately, the next thing you know, the guy leaves the safety net of the group setting, and wanders off alone at night, just asking for trouble!

And he takes the way to her house in the twilight,
in the evening, in the middle of the night
and in the darkness.
Proverbs 7:8-9 (NASV)

Solomon uses four different words to describe the night scene: "in the twilight...in the evening...in the middle of the night...in the darkness." He is obviously perplexed and upset that the young man would leave the group to go down a dark alley at night alone. Solomon looks down the street to see what lured the young man to leave the safety net of friends and go down the path of darkness. He sees at the end of the street a woman with honey dripping from her mouth.

There is a feeling of accountability and moral obligation when you are with others. Call it collective conscience. God has placed within human society, even in its most depraved condition, the natural desire to keep each other from making wrong choices. Our problem begins when we have a stubborn, independent spirit that makes us prone to wander down a dark path alone. Men, stay with the group. Don't wander off by yourself looking for dripping honey.

Set Up Some Role Models to Follow

Follow the steps of good men instead,
and stay on the paths of the righteous.
Proverbs 2:20

Guys, to avoid moral failure in our sex-saturated society, we need role models to follow. Stand on the wise counsel of successful men instead of falling for female flattery. We need heroes of the faith, men of integrity. One such role model comes from the Old Testament. He was a man who experienced all the things that might lead a man to "justify" having an affair. This man lost everything in a terrible mid-life crisis. Disease and financial ruin overcame him. His life got so bad that his wife advised him to curse God and die. Even his accountability group quit believing in him. However, Job didn't give in and seek comfort from low-commitment female companionship, though he certainly had opportunity. He said, "I made a covenant with my eyes not to look with lust at a girl" (Job 31:1, NIV). Would you be willing to make that same covenant now?

My brother, think of some man you know who is sexually pure, and ask him to help you become like him. If you don't know any such men, seek out a church in your area where leaders can help you be pure. Find a church that has an active men's ministry to provide you with opportunities to attend men's gatherings. There, you can be encouraged by solid Bible teaching and fellowship with other guys who want to rise above the moral fog of our day. Church leaders can help you find ways to serve others, and in so doing you will get beyond one of the root causes of sexual impurity: self absorption.

In Hong Kong, where we live, sexual temptation appears at every turn. There are sections of town to be avoided at night. The walls at subway stops are often plastered with advertisements featuring life-size women in bikinis. Foreign women seem to come to Hong Kong to make money selling themselves. The culture lends itself to sexual "openness." Yet in the middle of all of that, I remember Don Mock. Don is a retired oil executive and a godly grandfather. He loves his wife and is faithful to her. I see Don regularly, and I am guided by how he genuinely enjoys serving his wife. I want to follow in his steps.

There are good men out there. Find a few and follow them. Develop a band of brothers, three or four men who share honestly with each other about matters of the heart and hold each other accountable.

Guard Against Women Who Stroke Your Ego.

Wisdom will save you from…
the flattery of the adulterous woman.
Proverbs 2:16 (NIV)

Guys, we tend to gravitate toward women who say nice things about us, and women know that's the way guys are. We are so predictable. Praising us works every time. There are some women who have unmet emotional needs they are trying to fill by getting men's attention and flattering us. They are out to get something; the satisfaction of a longing look in a man's eye, hearing a man's voice say how beautiful they are, or an "A" on her flirt-ability report card when she returns to her girlfriends. These kinds of women are definitely not your best female friends.

Who can find a virtuous and capable wife?
She is worth more than precious rubies. Her husband
can trust her, and she will greatly enrich his life.
She will not hinder him but will help him all her life.
Proverbs 31:10–12

Your wife has emotional antennas that you don't have. They are invisible but they stick up right out of the top of her head. She knows when other women have inappropriate feelings toward you. Listen to what your wife says about other women around you, and your ego won't become inflated. Be open to her help. Ask for her help. She is a precious jewel. Listen to sweet talking women, and you'll get into trouble.

If you don't have a wife, I recommend you let God give you one. A good wife will cost you the great expense of becoming the kind of man whom a good woman would want to have, but she will be worth the cost. She will give you wisdom to overcome the flattery of other women.

Accountability by itself is not enough to keep us pure. You must not put the responsibility of your purity over onto other men or onto your wife. Own it, my friend.

Determine Beforehand in Your Heart What You Will Do.

Watch your heart with all diligence, for from it flow the springs of life. Proverbs 4:23 (NASV)

Don't let your heart stray away toward her. Don't wander down her wayward path. Proverbs 7:25

Purity is not a matter of following a set of rules or living within a plastic bubble of protection. It's a matter of maintaining a pure heart before God. Purity can only be a consistent part of your life when you love God so much that you hate doing things that displease him. If the holy fire that once burned within has now become ashes, return to your first love. Be a man of prayer, depending on the filling of God's Spirit to empower you to live victoriously in Jesus Christ.

Someone is knocking at the door. Open the door and let Him in. Unlock every room. Let Him move around in every chamber of your heart. Don't treat him as a guest, even a very honored guest. He is not a guest. He is the owner of the house. Give Him the keys and tell Him you recognize Him as owner. Are you still holding back that one hidden chamber of your heart? Give *that* to Jesus Christ as well. Your heart must be undividedly His. A divided heart will make you only half a man.

Let your heart be so full of desire to please God that you are repulsed by sexual immorality. Ask God to cleanse your heart and make you a man of holy passion for pleasing the Father. My father's favorite hymn is "Satisfied with Jesus." The song starts out saying, "I am Satisfied with Jesus. He has done so much for me." However, my father's favorite line is a personal life challenge by which he seeks to live. His life line comes at the end of the song: "Is my Master satisfied with me?" This challenge remains daily on my father's heart.

Above all, guard your heart. If your heart is set on unfaithfulness and illicit excitement, married sex will not satisfy you. At whatever point sexual pollution has entered your life, do away with it. End it! If the chains of habit have already wrapped themselves tightly around you, then get help. Decide now that you will have no part in it. Sexual impurity does not begin in the bedroom. It begins in the heart. Be a man in pursuit of God's own heart. God is holy. Let us be holy men of God.

If All Else Fails, Run.

So now my sons, listen to me. Never stray from what I am about to say: Run from her! Don't go near…
Proverbs 5:7-8

In Asia, where I live and frequently travel for work, there is a large industry centered on sexual entertainment for traveling men. The night sky is lit up with signs to lure in men. Even in the hotel room, the phone will ring. A soft, needy, female voice will say "Ni Hao. Ni Yao bu yao wo?" ("Don't you want me?") The girl sounds like she is calling from just outside the door. I have learned when checking in to the hotel, to always ask for a "quiet" room. That puts me away from the areas where sexual entertainment is the focus. Then when I enter the room, I unplug the phone from the wall. Men, there are people in this world who make their living by trying to get us to fail morally. Let's put them out of business. We must take the practical steps needed to purposefully distance ourselves from temptation. Run from her. Guys, let's get off our rear ends and get in shape. Let's run.

Often the greatest temptation is not from the sex industry. It is from women that you know from work, from the community where you live, the gym where you work-out, your wife's friends, or ladies at the church where you worship. If you are married, don't ever take the initiative to develop a one on one friendship with *any* of these ladies, even if it starts out only as friends. Friendship within the group context is fine, but one on one meetings will only lead to trouble.

If you are a single man, let your basis for relationships first be a long-term friendship in a group context. There you can both get a more accurate picture of what the other is like. Never use your position of authority at work to subtly pressure a female into being involved with you. If a female co-worker is pursuing you for casual recreational sex, let her know clearly you are not that kind of guy. Run.

Men, take inventory of how you are doing in this area. Put a check by each of these areas only if you are honestly and consistently doing it.

- I make a habit of asking, "What if my sister Wisdom were here?"
- I don't eat mystery meat.
- I can continue living as I am, and not die an old pervert.
- I have healthy group time with other guys, and don't wander off alone looking for temptation.
- I have moral men who keep me accountable for my sex life.
- I ignore it when a woman tugs at me with flirty, flattering words.
- I have determined in my heart that I will stay pure for God's sake.
- I realize my own weakness. I'm ready to run away when needed.

How many of the eight areas could you honestly answer yes? If you answered yes to four or less, you need to go to a mentor for guidance. Five or six yes answers mean that, after a few tweaks, you are well on your way toward enjoying who you are as a sexually pure man. If you answered all eight yes, ask your wife if she agrees with your answers! Still single?

Then pray for God to give you that precious jewel, and wait for her!

Remember, sexual purity is not achieved through a checklist. Purity is a matter of the heart. Let's go back to Mike Singletary, who was unfaithful to his wife during their engagement. He became so unsure of himself that he had to sleep with the light on. What happened to Mike after that? Mike came clean. He confessed to his wife and to God. His wife cried for a long time. He knew that he had deeply hurt the people he loved the most. He felt pain unlike any he had ever felt.

It was then that he asked for forgiveness. God began doing a work in his heart and life. Mike was becoming empty of self. His pride began dissolving in God's grace. The pain was immense. God's acceptance was incomparably sweet. There was a hole of pain in Mike's heart, which he began filling with God's wisdom for purity. He wrote, "Now God was filling the void in me that had so long been filled by my ego, by my sin, by the world. To this day I'm not entirely sure what happened, but I know I became a new man."[33]

HOW TO STAY SEXUALLY PURE AS A WOMAN

Sally was working on some personal issues in her life and asked her friends to help her. They took her to church with them each week. Sally realized worship met a deep need in her heart. She had struggled with some difficult relationships with boyfriends, and her self-image was out of whack. Her fiancé had broken up with her a few months earlier. She decided to forget the whole dating scene for a while, and just hang out with friends. She was enjoying her friends and some volunteer work she started doing at a community shelter. Then she happened to meet a fellow we'll just call

"Goober." That's just what he was, though he was handsome. She couldn't help but notice that Goober was better looking than her ex.

Sally and Goober really enjoyed spending time together, and before you know it they were dating exclusively. She bought new clothes to wear only on special nights out with him when she really wanted her features to be noticed. Over a romantic dinner, she leaned toward him, stroked the hair on his arm, and looked deeply into his eyes without saying a word. She could tell she was causing feelings to stir within him. Sally told Goob how much she admired his strong personality.

Her friends excitedly teased her about the new love in her life. Sally wanted to bring Goober around to meet her friends, but it was not a priority to him. He remained a mystery, and Sally's friends seldom saw her. Goober wanted to go to the beach and surf the waves on Sunday mornings. He liked to have Sally sit on the sand and watch him. Though Sally was a bit bored when she just had to sit there on the beach to keep him happy, from Sally's perspective, almost everything was great-sort of. They loved doing things together and enjoyed getting to know each other. What she didn't see was that she was gradually being changed. Her interest in God had gone away. She hadn't turned her back on God. Sally was just totally consumed with a real Goober.

She had gained some wisdom from her previous relationships and had made a vow to God that she would not sleep with a man again until she was married. She liked to tease Goober that the possibility of being intimate was there, but she really intended it to be only flirt without the frills. However, after some mild pressure and too many evenings watching movies together on his bed, she began sleeping with Goober. She assured herself it was all right because this time it was going to be forever.

Goober started talking to her about getting cosmetic surgery to enhance her appearance. She just laughed it off as a joke, but he kept bringing it up, saying she needed to lose weight and get surgery to improve her looks. She began noticing that Goober was not at all concerned with *her* interests or the people in *her* life. Too, whatever happened to the volunteer work she enjoyed so much? It was a thing of the past. She finally reconnected with her friends. Sobbing, Sally poured out her anguish and heartache to them.[34]

Let's suppose you were Sally's friend. You've listened to Sally share her frustrations. What would be your reaction? What would you say to her? What things about Goober would you help her see? Would you help her get out of her current relationship or tell her to stay in the relationship? What advice would you give her in future relationships? What changes does she need to make?

What biblical principles from Proverbs can help Sally and other ladies stay sexually pure? Though the following guidelines may seem a bit extreme at first, I challenge you ladies to give them a try for a few months. See your self-esteem improve. Watch the basis of your self-worth shift. No longer are you consumed with making a good impression with your voice and body. Instead you are blossoming as a person truly worth getting to know from the inside out. See how your inner cravings are no longer temporarily satisfied with hurtful relationships but with something far more satisfying and lasting.

Proverbs gives us a picture of a desperate housewife. She had legitimate needs, but was trying to fill them in illegitimate ways. This woman below makes Sally above look like a nun. Ladies, if your goal is sexually purity, this lady is a perfect example of exactly what not to do. Here's the check list on staying sexually pure as a woman.

Avoid Flattering Guys.

The desperate housewife said...

It's you I was looking for!
I came out to find you, and here you are!
Proverbs 7:15
(See also 2:16, 5:3, 7:5, 22:1)

She was stroking his ego just to get him to meet her needs. Saying flattering words isn't communication. It's manipulation. This lady's motives were obvious. Sometimes women flatter men without the improper motive of hoping for intimacy. However, flattery may lead to an improper relationship. Women, you must understand men. Men take flattery as a clear come-on. Seemingly innocent words can later lead to impure intimacy. It may start out as just well-meaning praise, but you find your praise for the man may lead to a relationship of nearly unbreakable emotional bond. He becomes addicted to your praise.

"The way to a man's heart is not through his stomach, but through his ego. Let a woman flatter him, make him feel important, indispensible, irresistible, and he will follow her anywhere."[35] It was the woman's flirty, suggestive words that shut down the man's clear thinking. "So she seduced him with her pretty speech" (Proverbs 7:21). Flirty flattery is exactly how to attract a Goober. Ladies, if you want to attract an insecure wimp, flattery will do it.

Remember Your Covenant to God.

This desperate lady of Proverbs was schizophrenic. In one minute, even if only in her imagination, she worships before God, promising to be a modest and respectable, God-fearing woman. A few minutes later she rushes home, changes into high-heels and a miniskirt, and puts on make-up so thick that she looks like a clown. She then runs out to stand on the street corner to take any guy who comes along. She sees one coming and says...

I've offered my sacrifices and just finished my vows.
Proverbs 7:14

She wants him to know she is a pious, good, churchgoing girl.

Church fellowship can go haywire if men and women allow the communion to become too close. Only God knows how many affairs have started after worship with words exchanged in the church parking lot. Church is a great place to meet your future mate but a terrible place to defile the things of God with improper sexual adventures. We've seen enough of that already. Don't pretend you are coming to church to seek God if you have really come in hopes of getting into an immoral relationship.

Sexual purity begins with making a covenant with God to be pure for Him as a temple of His Spirit. Ladies, never let it be said of you that "she...ignores the covenant she made before God" (Proverbs 2:17).

Be Honest with Yourself About the Path You are Setting.

Her feet go down to death; her steps lead straight to the grave. For she does not care about the path to life. She staggers down a crooked trail and doesn't even realize where it leads. Proverbs 5:5-6

Self deception is perhaps the central issue that locks people into sexual impurity's trap. We tell ourselves some reason why it is wrong for others but right for us. We are different. They will get burned by fire, but we can handle fire and not get burned. Even now, you may be saying "I can stop anytime I want to." Okay, then, stop now. If you find yourself unable to stop, then you must honestly admit you have a bigger problem than you can handle alone. Get help.

Notice that this lady *chose* the path leading to death. No one forced her. We each choose our life path. Road signs are clear (at least in the U.S.!) about where the road will take you. If you choose the path of sexual impurity, don't tell yourself it will lead to pure pleasure. Impure pleasure may be fun for a season, but choosing it is choosing a road that is clearly marked. It leads to death. What path are you following? If you keep going as you are going now, where will your habits lead you?

Dress for Success, Not for Sex.

Charm is deceptive, and beauty does not last;
but a woman who fears the Lord will be greatly praised.
Proverbs 31:30

"The woman approached him, dressed seductively and sly of heart" (Proverbs 7:10). She had painted herself and dolled-up her body to airbrush perfection. Lust had an aristocratic lady in its grip, reducing her to a sex-starved clown. In her heart was a plot to deceive men for personal gain.

Remember modern day Sally and her struggles with what's his name? Yes, he was a challenge, but was it entirely his fault? Did Sally have anything to do with the way things turned out? Sally purposefully wore clothes that were revealing and tight. The fellow got the idea that she was easy. She was asking for it. What should Sally have done in the way of wardrobe alteration? If Sally had dressed as a successful, confident, beautiful but discreet and capable woman, Goober might have thought, *This lady is not desperate. She knows herself. She expects me to get to know her, too. If I want an easy target, I better move on. She is not the one.*

I've traveled many places and have seen most continents of the world. In most countries, women are dressed with discretion and modesty. However in some countries this is not the case. Which country might get the designation of having the most seductively dressed women? It might be one of the countries of Europe, but then America would be a close second runner-up. After living outside the States for nearly two decades, it is shocking to go back to America occasionally and see what women, particularly young ladies, are wearing-or *not* wearing.

What are you wearing these days, ladies? What is your clothing saying to men?

A woman who is beautiful but lacks discretion
is like a gold ring in a pig's snout.
Proverbs 11:22

Be Careful What You Do With Your Body.

Look just how forward this woman of Proverbs was.

She threw her arms around him and kissed him.
Proverbs 7:10

Ladies, you must understand what even the smallest physical touch can do to a guy. A slight slap of his hand during conversation, a hand placed on his shoulder out of concern, a hug that pulls him to your breasts, a little finger jab at his side–to a guy these may seem like invitations to go further physically. A guy thinks you are flirting with him.

Woman, your body has the power to spark the vivid imagination of man. Be cautious in even seemingly innocent touch. Even if you are dating, you certainly do not want to see just how far you can go physically without going all the way. Reserve the intimate touch for marriage. Save your feminine, seductive skills for marital sex. Don't let physical flirting lead to extra-marital seduction.

Don't Hang Around Hoping for a Guy to Come Along.

This dolled-up lady was "often seen in the streets and markets, soliciting at every corner" (Proverbs 7:12). She positioned herself in a high traffic area. Some guys, like Goober, tend to go to areas where females may be hanging out, waiting for them. Ladies, do you find yourself going to places just to see what guys might be there? You may feel highly motivated to be intimate with a guy, but that need may be caused in part by some emptiness inside your heart. Deal with what's going on in your heart. Become a whole person, complete in Christ; then go about your everyday life. Become Ms. Right, and then Mr. Goober will avoid you, while Mr. Right may take notice of you. You won't have to advertise for the right kind of man to notice you. Are you going to hot-spots and looking available? Goober is there waiting for you. Let those days be gone forever.

Don't Go In a Bedroom With Someone Who Is Not Your Husband.

My bed is spread with colored sheets of finest linen imported from Egypt. I've perfumed my bed with myrrh, aloes, and cinnamon.
Proverbs 7:16-17

The Proverbs housewife was hoping for someone to come along into her bedroom. Modern day Sally made the mistake of watching movies on her boyfriend's bed.

In Florida, some young people removed a stop sign from an intersection just for fun. Soon a fatal accident happened at the intersection. The youth who removed the sign were held responsible for the deaths that occurred. Picture God handing you a big red stop sign. Put that sign outside the bedroom. Ignoring God's stop sign will destroy your life and the lives of others.

Stop Getting Into Disposable Relationships.

Come, let's drink our fill of love until morning. Let's enjoy each other's caresses, for my husband is not home.
Proverbs 7:18-19

This lady was so desperate that she risked her husband finding out. What if he were to return early from his trip? What if a neighbor told him what his wife was doing while he was gone? She was willing to chance losing her husband to gain a short-time pleasure.

"There is probably no greater satanic stronghold in our culture than the idea of disposable marriage."[36]

The tendency is to short-circuit the needed time to get to know each other as friends and just jump right in to romance. Microwave relationships wrapped in glittery plastic heat up quickly, but leave a bad taste in the mouth and are then discarded into the trash like food and plastic melted together.

Look back over Sally's situation in light of this checklist. Though Sally was not as obviously desperate like the housewife of Proverbs, she actually committed the same mistakes. She flattered Goober, deceived herself about the direction of the relationship, dressed provocatively instead of discreetly, was not careful with her bodily contact with him, kept his ego fed, let the pursuit of a man come before the pursuit of God, and went into his bedroom with him. Before she knew it, there she was disposing of one more serial lover.

Now ladies, you must look at yourself. Place a check by every one that is true for you.

- ☐ I avoid flattering guys.
- ☐ I remember my covenant before God to be sexually pure.
- ☐ I am honest with myself about the path my life is taking.
- ☐ I dress for success, not sex.
- ☐ I am careful with what I do with my body.
- ☐ I don't go to hang-outs hoping to get picked up by a guy.
- ☐ I don't go into a bedroom with a man who is not my husband.
- ☐ I am done with disposable relationships.

How many were you able to check? If you checked four or less, it would be good to share the things of your heart with someone who can help you. Five or six checks shows you are moving in the right direction, and seven means you should go reward yourself with the coffee of your choice. Eight means you need to be the one writing this section of the book!

GUYS AND GALS, CHOOSE PURITY

Whether you are male or female, the message is the same. Choose to be sexually pure. It is not enough to gain mere knowledge or to check off a list. You are only as wise as the amount of knowledge you actually apply to your lifestyle. With all his knowledge about wisdom, we still cannot say that Solomon, the writer of the proverbs we now study, lived a wise life. He ended his life foolishly. He gave himself over as a captive to his own lust. He forgot the best interests of the people, and nearly wrecked his own government. He died worn out by excessive self indulgence, leaving behind an impoverished treasury, a discontented people, and a tottering empire. He died as he sometimes lived—self-centered.[37] Solomon wrote about the miserable end results of his carefree sexual pleasure.

I said to myself, "Come now, let's give pleasure a try.
Let's look for the 'good things' in life." But I found that
this too was meaningless...
What good does it do to seek only pleasure?
I...had many beautiful concubines. I had everything a
man could desire! Anything I wanted, I took. I did not
restrain myself from any joy ...But as I looked at
everything...it was all so meaningless.
It was like chasing the wind. There was nothing really
worthwhile anywhere.
Ecclesiastes 2:1-2,8,10-11

Sexual impurity leads to a meaningless existence. Is that what you want? Choose today to be sexually pure. You'll be glad you did. Choose a life of confidence and joy by choosing sexual purity. Then share this decision with others who can encourage you and hold you accountable. You will become free from the captivity of sexual sin, and enjoy developing into the person God created you to be. Enjoy sex the way God created it to be enjoyed–within the safety and lifelong commitment of marriage. Within marriage, self-giving sex is pure pleasure. As humans, we desire sexual satisfaction. It is a normal, healthy, biblical desire given to us by God. The presence of that desire is not the same as the privilege to satisfy that desire however we want. The way to experience the sexual and emotional fulfillment you desire is within the safety of marriage.

BANK ON IT!

Follow God's Plan of Economy!

Much of the book of Proverbs is Solomon writing to give his son advice. It reminds me of how touched my heart was when I read Charlie Shedd's *Letters to Phillip.* If you have a young man soon to be on his own, I advise you to find a copy of Charlie's book and read it. For your daughter, read *Letters to Karen.* In that spirit, the message here on money is straight from me to our two sons, who will soon stand on their own feet financially. It's from my heart to theirs, but the rest of you can listen in as well. Solomon's advice to his son is good advice for my sons. Regardless of whether you are young or old, male or female, it's good advice for you too. I invite you to listen in to my financial advice to our sons.

Joshua and Jonathan, as your father, one of the primary

goals of my life is to bless you and mold you into the men God wants you to become. You've heard me talk about wise use of money many times as you were growing up, and you've seen your parents' lifestyle. We are stewards, not owners, of all the possessions that God has entrusted to our use during our time on this earth. I now bless you with a concise summary of the financial principles found in the book of Proverbs. Take them to heart, and you will avoid so many serious financial pitfalls that detour many young adults. Apply these God-given practices now and in the future as you start your family. You will then see God grow your resources into a base of wealth used for His Kingdom's sake. It will be a great joy for your mother and me to watch what God does through your lives and the resources He gives you.

I know that East Asia will always be a big part of who you two men are, having grown up there. Let's start with a story from that part of the world.

There was once a fellow who, with his dad, farmed a little piece of land. Several times a year they would load up the old ox-drawn cart with vegetables and go into the nearest city to sell their produce. Except for their name and the patch of ground, father and son had little in common. The old man believed in taking it easy. Usually in a hurry, the boy was the go-getter type.

One morning, bright and early, they hitched up the ox to the loaded cart and started on the long journey. The son figured that if they went faster, kept going all day and night, they'd make market by early the next morning. As a result, he kept prodding the ox with a stick, urging the beast to get a move on.

"Take it easy, son," said the old man. "You'll last longer."

"But if we get to market ahead of the others, we'll have a better chance of getting good prices," argued the son.

No reply. Dad just pulled his hat down over his eyes and fell asleep on the seat. Itchy and irritated, the young man kept goading the ox to walk faster. However, the ox's stubborn pace refused to change.

Four hours and four miles later down the road, they came to a little house. The father woke up, smiled and said, "Here's your uncle's place. Let's stop in and say hello."

"But we've lost an hour already," complained the hot shot.

"Then a few more minutes won't matter. My brother and I live so close, yet we see each other so seldom," the father answered slowly.

The boy fidgeted and fumed while the two old men laughed and talked for almost an hour. On the move again, the man took his turn leading the ox. As they approached a fork in the road, the father led the ox to the right.

"The left is the shorter way," said the son.

"I know it," replied the old man, "but this way is much prettier."

"Have you no respect for time?" the young man asked impatiently.

"Oh, I respect if very much! That's why I like to use it to look at beauty and enjoy each moment to the fullest."

The winding path led through graceful meadows, wildflowers, and along a rippling stream–all of which the young man missed as he churned within, preoccupied and boiling with anxiety. He didn't even notice how lovely the sunset was that day.

Twilight found them in what looked like a huge, colorful garden. The old man breathed in the aroma, listened to the bubbling brook, and pulled the ox to a halt. "Let's sleep here," he sighed.

"This is the last trip I'm taking with you," snapped

the son. "You're more interested in watching sunsets and smelling flowers than in making money!"

"Why, that's the nicest thing you've said in a long time," smiled the dad. A couple of minutes later he was snoring–as his boy glared back at the stars. The night dragged slowly. The son was restless.

Before sunrise the young man hurriedly shook his father awake. They hitched up and went on. About a mile down the road they happened on another farmer– a total stranger– trying to pull his cart out of a ditch.

"Let's give him a hand," whispered the old man. "And lose more time?" The boy exploded.

"Relax, son. You might be in a ditch sometime yourself. We need to help others in need–don't forget that." The boy looked away in anger.

It was almost eight o'clock that morning by the time the other cart was back on the road. Suddenly, a great flash split the sky, followed by what sounded like thunder. Beyond the hills, the sky grew dark.

"Looks like a big rain in the city," said the old man.

"If we had hurried, we'd be almost sold out by now," grumbled the son.

"Take it easy. You'll last longer, and you'll enjoy life so much more," counseled the kind old gentleman.

It was late afternoon by the time they got to the hill overlooking the city. They stopped and stared down at it for a long, long time. Neither of them said a word. Finally, the young man put his hand on his father's shoulder and said, "I see what you mean, Dad."

They turned their cart around and began to roll slowly away from what had the day before been the city of Hiroshima.[38]

Joshua and Jonathan,

There is a way that seems right to a man,
but in the end it leads to death.
Proverbs 14:12 (NIV)

So many lives have been ruined by focusing on making money. It's what seems right. We want to provide the best for our families and own houses in the better neighborhoods. We want to pull up to the stop light driving the car that everyone turns to look at. The desire for money drives many people to become workaholics and ruin their own health and families in the process. They become oppressed and wretched slaves of the almighty dollar.

Instead of living for money, follow the timeless financial principles set out by wise Solomon. Here they are.

Go for Quality of Life over Gaining Wealth

All the days of the oppressed are wretched,
but the cheerful heart has a continual feast.
Better a little with the fear of the Lord
than great wealth with turmoil.
Better a meal of vegetables where there is love than a
fattened calf with hatred. Proverbs 15:15-17 (NIV)

My sons, don't center your life on money. Cultivate happiness and share your happiness over meals with family and friends. A money-focused life will cause you to miss too many meals away from home at meetings. Instead, you will often eat at home with a cheerful heart, and people will like to be around a cheerful person like you. Friends will enjoy eating leisurely meals with you; much like you and the Koreans did together in a country where the people seem to spend at least twenty-five percent of their income hosting friends at nice meals together. You will likely be like your mother, who enjoys having continual feasts in our home when we have company or even when it's just our family.

There's something more to life than just earning a living, and that is living itself! Don't buy into the American rat race that says time is money. No way! Time is life! Life is to be lived. Money is to be used to help us live the lifestyle God wants us to live. Don't be a rat! Get a life! Live! Take time to go visit your brother and his family instead of rushing to make another buck. Take the time to help a man pull his ox out of the ditch even if it means getting to the market late. Living for money will not afford you the time to enjoy life.

Live for the Lord. Put him first in your career choice. Do not choose a career based on how much money you can earn doing it. You may find money, but have only turmoil deep down in your soul. If money rules your life, it brings tension to your relationships with others. Find out what God wants you to do with your life and trust Him to provide what you need to do it. It really *is* that simple, and He really is that dependable.

Go for quality of relationships over making money. Fill your family with the love your mother and I poured out onto you. Don't worry if you don't have expensive things. Your mother and I didn't even have a bed to sleep on when we got married, but God soon provided one. Over the years we have lived on whatever He provided, and He has been faithful. Do not love things and use people. Love people and use things.

Vegetables are much cheaper and better for you than expensive meat! You guys have grown up on fresh vegetables from the outdoor market, prepared with your mother's heart full of love. When vegetables are eaten with your family together around a table where love and laughter is shared, you are the richest of men! Life is good! By the way, don't forget to follow my example and wash the dishes after every meal your wife cooks. Talk about bringing love into a relationship - that will do it!

Seek Character Development More than Financial Growth

Do not wear yourself out to get rich; have
the wisdom to show restraint.
Cast but a glance at riches, and they are gone,
for they will surely sprout wings and fly off to the sky
like an eagle. Proverbs 23:4-5 (NIV)

When you are blessed with money, it's a test to see how you will manage it. It is a test of your character. Show restraint. Make financial decisions slowly-never on impulse and never without consulting your wife. Learn to be content with a little, and later, when you are blessed with much, don't forget your humble roots and the free easy feeling you had when you were content with just a little. *Don't increase your spending just because you have more to spend! Always spend less than you make!*

Give me neither poverty nor riches,
but give me only my daily bread. Other wise, I
may have too much and disown you and say,
'Who is the Lord?' Or I may become poor and steal,
and so dishonor the name of my God.
Proverbs 30:8-9 (NIV)

Your contentment must not be based on how much you have. Tomorrow you may have less and then you will not be content. Find your contentment in your relationship with the Lord. He never disappoints. One day the stock market is at a five year high, and a month later it has cratered to rock bottom. However, He is still there, the solid Rock. Stand on Him. The world may value people according to how much they have, but you are not of the world. Let God be the one who puts a value on you. He put the price tag on you when He died on the cross for you. He says you are priceless to Him. He says that about each person, regardless of his bank balance. You should do the same.

Aim at gaining wisdom, not merely making money.

How much better to get wisdom than gold,
to choose understanding rather than silver.
Proverbs 16:16 (NIV)

Of what use is money in the hand of a fool,
since he has no desire to get wisdom?
Proverbs 17:16 (NIV)

Gold there is, and rubies in abundance,
But lips that speak knowledge are a rare jewel.
Proverbs 20:15 (NIV)

Give God First Place with Your Finances

Honor the Lord with your wealth,
With the first-fruits of all your crops:
Then your barns will be filled to over flowing
And your vats will brim over with new wine.
Proverbs 3:9-10 (NIV)

Joshua and Jonathan, you may remember me telling you about when I was a nineteen year old pastor of a new church. I felt God leading me to share the gospel and gather believers together in a small community on Lake o' the Pines in North East Texas about thirty minutes away from East Texas Baptist University, the school where I was studying. We started the church at Pop's Landing, a small bait store and bar on the lake. In the summers, I would leave the dorm and live out on the edge of the lake in a small cabin. One summer, there was to be a camp for teenagers nearby, and we had three teenagers in our new congregation. By that time, I had turned twenty, so I was not one of the three!

It seemed clear to me that those three teenagers needed to go to summer camp. However, their parents supposedly didn't have the fifty dollars needed to send them. I didn't either if I wanted to eat. At the beginning of every month, as soon as I was paid, I gave at least ten percent of my total income to the Lord at church. It's a lifelong habit. In God's plan of economy it is the starting point after which real giving begins. Nevertheless, it took real faith to give when nothing was left after doing so! That summer, after praying about those three teenagers, I did what was impressed on my heart. I wrote out a personal check for one hundred fifty dollars, and drove those kids to camp. I had no idea how I was going to eat for the rest of the month, but I had done the right thing.

During that week I was out in the yard clearing some woods around my rented cabin to keep critters away. An elderly lady I had never seen before pulled up in a big, white, four-door Ford LTD. She got out, walked up to me and said, "Are you Matthew Nance, Pastor of South Side Baptist Church?"

"Yes, I am."

"God told me to give this to you." She handed me two hundred dollars cash! Then she just turned, got in her car, and left! I went inside, knelt down with tears flowing, and praised God! Then I went to the store, bought groceries, cooked (if you can call it that!), and ate. I had planned to keep my giving a secret, until God surprised me by returning the money plus a bonus! I just had to brag on Him! The next Sunday as I preached at church, I told the people about what had happened.

Giving in our church began to go up significantly after that. Little financial miracles began occurring as money was freed up to meet each other's needs. The poor people in that community began to experience a financial lift as they followed God's plan of economy by helping each other. Summer came around again, and we had more youth going to camp. Those youth who needed help to go were assisted by a surplus of church funds. I never saw that elderly lady again. Yes, there are angels all around!

The lesson I learned that day has stuck with me for life. *You cannot out-give God.* Left to my own self-centeredness, I might become a greedy, stingy man, but God has moved me to become a giver. Give to the Lord first-as soon as you receive money. He will bless you in return more than you will bless Him by helping others. In God's plan of economy, money is not meant to be hoarded or to be stagnant. It gets stinky that way. It is meant to flow. Your mother is by nature a giver. She and I enjoy a lifestyle of giving our first-fruits to the Lord, then being generous to others. Although it was not our goal, the result has been many blessings flowing back to us in return.

Earn Money in a Way That Has Integrity

There are all kinds of ways to get rich, and not all of them are illegal. However, do all of these methods honor God? Does making money that way develop a good reputation for you among men?

A Man will do wrong for a piece of bread.
Proverbs 28:21 (NIV)

We've lived in some places where there have been many people around us who were literally scrambling for survival. Joshua and Jonathan, you've seen with your own eyes what men will do just to have food to eat. Remember the street person who ran right past me, grabbed some lady's cell phone and took off running so fast he left his hole-y shoes behind? I've often wondered what I would stoop to if I were as hungry as some people whom we have seen. Don't ever let the cash in your wallet get so low that you are tempted to gain money in dishonest ways in order to make ends meet. Keep a reserve of money, even if it means doing manual labor on the side to earn it. Sweat is good for you.

Food gained by fraud tastes sweet to a man,
but he ends up with a mouth full of gravel.
Proverbs 20:17 (NIV)

A fortune made by a lying tongue
is a fleeting vapor and a deadly snare.
Proverbs 21:6 (NIV)

Better a poor man whose walk is blameless
than a rich man whose ways are perverse.
Proverbs 28:6 (NIV)

Earning money is a necessary part of modern life. However, remember, it's not how much money you make, but how you make it. Earn it honestly. Work hard. Sweat. Work smart. Think. Cooperate with others. In the work arena, create an atmosphere of honesty, excellence, and integrity. Give your work your very best for the sake of a job well done, for the glory of God, and for the honor of your name as a Nance man.

Develop a Stable Life and Income, Then Buy or Build a House

Finish your outdoor work and get your fields ready;
after that, build your house.
Proverbs 24:27 (NIV)

You shouldn't buy a house if there's a good chance you won't be living in the place for at least five years. It costs a lot of money to get into and out of a house, and the value of the house won't appreciate that much in fewer than five years. You shouldn't buy a house until your lives are stable in one place and you have solid, dependable income. Don't set your sights on a house that is out of your league.

Live frugally in order to prepare for putting at least twenty percent down payment on your first home purchase. Frugality is already in your DNA. Your great-grandmother Nance was so frugal she could squeeze a penny until you heard it cry! She was tight with her money; tighter than bark on a tree! However, she gave generously to those in need. She gave your mother and me our first washing machine.

Once the time is right to buy a house, don't be afraid to do so. When you are stable in your work and your place of living, buy or build a house. It's better than renting, and can be a decent long term investment. Get your fields ready and then build your house.

Avoid Debt

The rich rule over the poor,
and the borrower Is servant to the lender.
Proverbs 22:7 (NIV)

You guys have done great in this area so far. That's partly because you saw the example of your parents. We are highly committed to debt-free living. He who is financially free is free indeed!

Another reason why you have not had a problem with debt is that you grew up in cash based societies. People either paid cash, or they didn't buy. You will more than likely end up living long term in the United States. As you learn of the financial habits of people in the States, you will feel tension. The savings rate in many Asian countries is at least thirty percent. In 2005 in the United States, according to CNN Headline News, the savings rate was a negative one point two percent. That means Americans are somehow spending more than one hundred and one percent of their income!

Joshua and Jonathan, you will feel pressure to go into debt. It's not for you. Being free of debt relieves all kinds of stress! Just leave the credit cards alone. One card that doubles as a debit and credit card is enough for emergency use and for purchasing things requiring a card. Just use it very sparingly and pay it off in full at the end of every month.

You will be graduating from university debt free! You've worked for your own spending money. We've invested carefully and worked hard, and your Grandparents have helped, all for you to be ready for life debt free. Borrow money, and you become a servant to the lender. One of the best things you can do for yourself financially is to stay as you are now–debt free.

Debt has become a modern addiction. Here are two examples to show you how crazy and foolish it is to use credit cards.

Elza is thirty years old. She has 3,500 dollars to pay on her credit card, at 18% interest. She decides to stop charging anything more on her card. However, she can only afford to pay the minimum twenty dollars per month toward her debt. How old will she be when she has that credit card paid off? The answer? Seventy! The solution would have been for her never to have used the credit card in the first place.

Case Study number two: Jack and Jill need a washing machine. They go to Sears without checking the sales ads and charge a $399 machine on credit at 18%. Paying the minimum of $35 per month, how much will they pay for their machine? The answer? 1,400 dollars! A laundry mat would have been much cheaper. Jack and Jill should have washed their clothes at fifty cents a load, saved the $35 per month until they had the cash, then continued to wait until the machine went on sell for $350! Then they can take the Sears ad to a competitor who promises to beat all competitor prices by $25! They might have been able to pay just $325 for the same machine! Just think what all they could have done with the 1,075 dollars they wasted on credit and impatience!

While we are on the subject of debt, Joshua, realize that if you counter-sign a loan with someone else as a way of "helping" them, you are no longer debt free. Legally, Jonathan, that debt is your responsibility, and it will become a burden to you. Solomon reminds us repeatedly:

A man lacking in judgment strikes hands in pledge
and puts up security for his neighbor.
Proverbs 17:18 (NIV)
see also 11:15,20:16,22:26-27,25:14,27:13

Be Generous Not Greedy.

A greedy man brings trouble to his family.
Proverbs 15:27 (NIV)

A greedy man stirs up dissension,
but he who trusts in the Lord will prosper.
Proverbs 28:25 (NIV)

A stingy man is eager to get rich
and is unaware that poverty awaits him.
Proverbs 28:22 (NIV)

It was announced that there would be a race for land. Starting at sun-up, the runners began. They knew that at sundown they must return to the place where they started, and they would be given all the land they could encircle by continuous running. To stop running would disqualify a person. Most all the runners started out too fast and received no land because they started walking. one man was determined to get for himself the most land he could, so he ran all day and returned just as the sun was setting. He immediately fell over and died from exhaustion! In the end, all the land he needed was about six feet–for burial!

Greed is a real killer! There's a far better way of life!

One man gives freely, yet gains even more; Another withholds unduly, but comes to poverty. A generous man will prosper; He who refreshes others will himself be refreshed. Proverbs 11:24-25 (NIV)

A generous man will himself be blessed, for he shares his food with the poor. Proverbs 22:9 (NIV)

Your great-grandpa Padgett was a chemical engineer for Exxon in Baytown, Texas. Though he was not an ordained pastor, he taught the Bible nearly every Sunday for decades. I was only able to visit him every few months, but each time I went to his house, he pulled out his Bible teaching charts and gave me a summary of the things God was teaching him.

Grandpa made a habit of generous giving. In the tithe envelope at church, he put in ten percent of his income given by check. He wanted to be an example to others in supporting the church budget. However, beyond the tithe, he also put much more into the offering plate in cash so that the church leaders would not know who had given the money. For his giving beyond the tithe, he wanted God alone to get the glory, not he himself. He also did not want people to try to enforce the golden rule: he who has the gold rules! Without letting others know, he often gave to many people in need. After he died, we found a notebook full of the names of those he had helped, with the amount by each name, followed by the word, "forgiven."

I thank God that when I married, I not only gained a great wife, but I was also blessed with a wonderful Grandpa. Solomon and Grandpa would have gotten along with each other really well! Maybe right now they are getting to know each other!

Make and Follow a Careful Investment Plan for the Long-Term

The plans of the diligent lead to profit
as surely as haste leads to poverty.
Proverbs 21:5 (NIV)

In the house of the wise are stores of food and oil,
but a foolish man devours all he has.
Proverbs 21:20 (NIV)

Dishonest money dwindles away,
but he who gathers money little by little makes it grow.
Proverbs 13:11 (NIV)

Notice the key words of the ancient, wise money manager.

Plan
Be Diligent Store Gather
Little by Little
Make it Grow

God is honored by the way we use our finances. He is not necessarily honored by a vow to remain poor. He is more concerned about what we do with what we have, not how much we have. The Bible instructs us to invest, and to do so wisely. If we just stick it under the mattress, we are not being responsible stewards. The Lord owns the cattle on a thousand hills. Whether he has entrusted you with ten of those cows or a hundred of them, He does not want those cows to starve and die. He wants you to make sure those cattle are healthy, reproducing, and resulting in income.

There is a simple plan that will help you become financially independent before you are forty five, even if your monthly income is not all that great. The plan will generate more than one million dollars of wealth for you. A million dollars won't be all that much by the time you are in your forties! However, by following the plan, you will have set a life-long pattern of proper investing that will carry you well into old age. Here's the plan:

1. Invest a consistent amount every month
2. Give your investment time to grow
3. Keep an eye on the return from your investment, making adjustments as needed
4. Use the resulting wealth in a lifestyle that honors God.

Here's an example. Let's say you graduate from university and begin working full time. You begin investing from the income of whatever work you are doing. You decide to invest just two dollars per day; that's sixty dollars per month. You set up an automatic monthly withdrawal of that amount from your bank account into an investment account at a brokerage company.

Through the brokerage account, you invest in Exchange Traded Funds rated by the brokerage firm as smart buys. ETFs are mutual funds that trade like stocks. Many ETFs are index funds. They simply follow whatever the U.S. stock market or a certain international market or sector is doing as a whole. Historically, since inception, the average annual return of the U.S. stock market has been about 10.7%. That's much better than you'll get at a bank! Many international ETFs bring much better than 20% per year. Let's say your ETFs average 20% per year return.

At 20% annual return on investment, sixty dollars invested each month from age twenty three to age forty three will result in just over a million dollars!

Not bad for just two dollars a day! Another way to build wealth is through carefully purchased rental property. Your goal would be to provide clean, affordable housing to others. It's important to buy at the right price, in a good location that appreciates in value, then place the property into the hands of a local property manager who selects good renters. The property can actually pay for itself over time, then because of appreciation in value, you can sell it for much more than you *didn't ever really pay for it!* Joshua and Jonathan, I'll be glad to guide you as you get started investing your money. There are many ways to develop multiple streams of income.

Be a wise manager who doesn't just stick money under the mattress. Make a plan. Diligently follow your plan over time. Watch the money grow little by little. Above all, use your wealth in a way that honors God. It all belongs to Him.

Live Right! You Will Experience a Financial Redemptive Lift!

The wealth of the wise is their crown,
but the folly of fools yields folly.
Proverbs 14:24 (NIV)

Humility and fear of the Lord
bring wealth and honor and life.
Proverbs 22:4 (NIV)

Though it is not always the result in every case, it is true that righteous living tends toward prosperity. How is this so? How many people do you know who are closely following the Lord but are still throwing their money away on drunkenness, sexual affairs, shady business deals in illegal or unwholesome industries, gambling, and the like? When people live a God-centered life, their priorities change. Their habits change, including how they spend money. The result is that their money flows into things that bless people, not burn them. Those who live a self-centered life instead of a God centered life find that their money is actually a curse. When you use money with integrity, you position yourself to be blessed by God.

Don't Try to Make Others Think You Have More Money than You Do!

A rich man may be wise in his own eyes,
but a poor man who has discernment sees through him.
Proverbs 28:11 (NIV)

As humans, we tend to admire the rich and believe they somehow are of more real value than those who are not rich. We flock to the rich and avoid the poor. We believe the rich are rich because they are wiser and smarter than others. This leads us to give other people the impression we have more than we do.

Like clouds and wind without rain
is a man who boasts of gifts he does not give.
Proverbs 25:14 (NIV)

There is refreshing strength in being "real," not pretending to be something you are not. And that's especially important when it comes to finances.

There is one who pretends to be rich, but has nothing;
another pretends to be poor, but has great wealth.
Proverbs 13:7 (NIV)

We think, "*Even if I cannot attain wealth, the least I can do is make other people think I have!*" We want other people to know how generous we supposedly are to those less blessed!

You guys have gone to international schools where most of your classmates were the kids of very wealthy businessmen. Because of the locations of foreigners' housing, you have always grown up living in neighborhoods of the nation's elite. You've never believed the "missionaries live in grass huts" myth! It would appear to those around you as you grew up that you were wealthy. Despite those appearances, you personally are not wealthy at present. One of your key challenges as a young adult will be to settle the issue in your mind that your value before God and others has nothing to do with your bank balance, the size of your house, and the model of your car. If you fail at settling this issue, you will never be content. You will always want more.

The millionaire John D. Rockefeller was asked one time, "How much does it take to satisfy a man completely?"

He said, "It takes a little bit more than what he has."[39]

Joshua and Jonathan, do you want to be truly satisfied? Know that you are totally loved and accepted by God through Jesus Christ. Bank on that, and don't try to live a shallow lifestyle of appearing wealthy for the sake of showing others your supposed worth. The good life exists only when we stop looking for a better one.

If you are not yet blessed with wealth, instead of trying to appear wealthy, become content with God as the center of your life, not money, and consider the advantages of a simple lifestyle.

A man's riches may ransom his life,
but a poor man hears no threat.
Proverbs 13:8 (NIV)

You can bank on God's plan of economy. Here's the next part of that plan.

Use Your Resources to Fight Injustice and Poverty

Why are the poor poor? Reasons for poverty include laziness (Proverbs 10:4, 19:15), useless pleasure seeking (Proverbs 21:17), alcoholism and gluttony (Proverbs 23:21), having an unteachable spirit (Proverbs 13:18), being full of hot air but not applying yourself (Proverbs 14:23), unwise, impulsive use of money (Proverbs 21:5), and injustice (Proverbs 13:23). Scripture is clear: ignoring the poor, making fun of them, or taking advantage of them–all are insults to God.

He who mocks the poor shows contempt for their Maker.
Proverbs 17:5 (NIV)

He who oppresses the poor to increase his wealth
and he who gives to the rich – both come to poverty.
Proverbs 22:16 (NIV)

Many who have never known hunger assume the poor are poor because they are lazy. We look at the poor and say, "If they'd just work hard, they could change their lifestyle." Laziness is one of many possible causes, but those who make such quick judgments on the poor have never lived long term among poor people. They've never attempted to truly understand the unjust systems of the world that continue to oppress the poor. Joshua and Jonathan, you have been to

Africa and India. You have lived among people struggling just to have food to eat for the day. You realize that the greatest cause of poverty is not the laziness of the poor.

Poverty continues because the poor are locked into circumstances which they are not able to control. No one has given them a chance at a different way of life. In the most poverty stricken areas of the world, this is painfully evident. There, the rich people clearly control the poor. Opportunities for enterprise, employment, and small business start up loans are given to those who already have money, not to the poor. Very seldom are attempts made to train and coach the poor in starting income-producing small businesses.[40]

Joshua and Jonathan, you and I have directly seen how thousands of poor people scramble in attempt to find any kind of work. They would gladly work if they only could find a job. Many poor people have genuinely given it their best to find work, but after years of fruitless struggle, they end up giving up. Your trip to India showed you the utter poverty of the second most populated country of the world. The smell of poverty may still be in you nostrils.

Are the poor unable to pull out of poverty because of lack of education? That may be a part of it. Education requires money and parents who value their children becoming educated. Poor children may have neither and may grow up to become like their parents. However many poor people are actually very intelligent and highly motivated.

We tend to see ourselves as superior to those who are not as well off as we are. We feel like we've done things right and they haven't. Sometimes we make jokes about them and laugh at the way they talk, the way they dress and walk, or how they drive a fancy, low-rider Cadillac, but still live in a dilapidated shack.

One main reason why the poor cannot break out of the

poverty cycle is because they are a part of a system that does not allow them to leave poverty. The rich and middle class have locked the poor into positions of lower service and have not provided them with opportunities to progress. This is called oppression. It is injustice, and it's happening all over the world.

A poor man's field may produce abundant food,
but injustice sweeps it away.
Proverbs 13:23 (NIV)

It's not a new problem. Even back in wise man Solomon's day, he was admonishing God's people to stop oppressing the poor.

A poor man pleads for mercy, but a rich man
answers harshly. Proverbs 18:23 (NIV)

If a man shuts his ear to the cry of the poor,
he too will cry out and not be answered.
Proverbs 21:13 (NIV)

He who is kind to the poor lends to the Lord,
and He will reward him for what he has done.
Proverbs 19:17 (NIV)

Blessed is he who is kind to the needy.
Proverbs 14:21 (NIV)
See also 22:9, 23:10, 28:3

My sons, I implore you. Look at people through God's eyes. He loves every person, regardless of the status the world may assign to them. Every person is God's own handiwork, and "He don't make no junk!"

Rich and poor have this in common;
The Lord is the Maker of them all.
Proverbs 22:2 (NIV)

I have seen both of you habitually help those in need, and I have been moved to tears of joy with how kind-hearted you are. Joshua and Jonathan, I challenge you to make your life count for fighting injustice and poverty in the world today. It is not an easy fight, a quick fight, or even a popular one, but it is what God expects of His children.

Be wise in how you help the poor. If you give a hungry person money, he may use it improperly. It is better to give him fish to eat. However, tomorrow he is still hungry and hoping you will feed him again. The best way is to teach him how to fish. Then he gains dignity and is free from dependence on you to feed him. Call the attention of other believers to the plight of the poor, and train other believers in how to help the poor break out of the cycle of poverty by gaining new thought processes and life-skills.

A true lift out of poverty will only be possible as believers accept responsibility to do something about the world's injustice and oppression. We must be moved to do more than just give money to charity organizations. We must get our hands dirty and relate directly to the poor, genuinely accepting them as fellow humans, sharing the Good News with them, letting the gospel rearrange their lives, and training them in the life skills they need. The result will often be a financial redemptive lift.

Poverty is not best solved through money. The most charitable thing we can do for the poor is to give them hope through a new life in Jesus Christ and, at the same time, teach them the skills they need to make it in life. Poverty is best solved through work, and many poor people, though not all, are eager to work.

The laborer's appetite works for him; His hunger drives him on. Proverbs 16:26 (NIV)

In the 1990's, I spent two unforgettable weeks in a small village in the Philippines. Waters were released from a dam on Luzon Island. The poor village below the dam found that most of their land was now five feet below water level and would remain that way. The poor had been oppressed once again and no one cared.

Believers in the village prayed about what to do and then they obeyed what God said. They formed a fish farm cooperative! This was a perfect solution to using the land they loved, which was now primarily covered with water. Four men were placed in each farm. Two men worked each farm by day and two by night. Several farms were started. They raised so many fish that the little church invited the entire village to come worship every Sunday. After worship they served free fish!

Many men in the village believed in Jesus, found joy replacing their grief, and joined one of the fish farms! The church became financially blessed, as each farm gave at least 10% of its income as well as 10% of its fish! So the church decided to buy jeepneys to provide free bus service for anyone in the village to go to and from the market each day!

A tragedy had struck, but God's people had turned it into a way to share the good news of new life in Jesus Christ, train others to meet their own needs through practicing a new skill, and bless those around them.

That, my sons, is God's exciting plan of economy!

Joshua and Jonathan, I love you guys very much!

Daddy

DO IT RIGHT!

Finding the Right Course of Action Every Time

I usually know what to do, or at least I think I do. Seldom do I find myself in a situation where I am at a loss of which direction to take. We each pride ourselves in being able to make good choices and determine our own future. We enjoy the pleasing, if not delusional, sensation that we are in charge of our own destiny. "I'm in control here." This feeling is a part of the human condition. Psychologists call it overconfidence. That day in March of 2004, God made it clear to me that my life was out of my control. Three of the most difficult months of my life followed that day. God used that season of life to set my heart on a different path.

It started when we were sharing the message of Christ broadly and boldly, pushing back darkness with the light of the gospel in a creative access country. From professionals to middle school students and peasant farmers, people from many walks of life heard the good news of God's love for the first time and found a relationship with Him through believing in Jesus Christ. It was a time of spiritual harvest and blessing, but not everyone liked the methods used to share the Gospel or the resulting changes taking place in the city. Simple house churches had sprung up here and there, and the status quo was being seriously threatened.

Several key co-workers had been missing for a few days, and strange men were answering the phone saying these co-workers would come back in a few days after they returned from a "trip." Why had they not told us they were leaving? We knew these people had been taken in for questioning and unusual treatment. Then the phone call came. Close friends called to say they had been questioned, and the authorities were coming that afternoon to take us in as well. We consulted our supervisors, who ordered us to leave the country immediately. We resisted, but had no choice.

When we left home on that Tuesday, I thought it would be just for a few days–a week at the most. But as it turns out, I never was able to go back. After a few weeks, the investigation of the work seemed to die down, and people were being released. However, authorities had gathered enough information to know they wanted to take me in. In order to avoid that, yet allow our boys to finish the school year, it was decided that Cheryl and the boys would return back to our city. I would have to stay outside the country.

The boys were followed to school every day. Authorities attempted to come to their school to question people about our family's activities. Cheryl had a few plain clothed investigators hovering over her every move as if they were guardian angels. They kept asking, "When is your husband coming back?" I was asking the same thing. I spent three months away from home, and it was not by my own choice. I am a homebody. It's against my nature to be away from home even one night. Day after day I cried. I sank lower and lower into despair. Why had God allowed *me* to be away from *my* family? Why couldn't I go back to *my* house? Didn't God know *my* work was important? My anger with God escalated to an irrational point where I clearly did not know anymore what to do with myself.

That's when I showed up on the door step of an old friend in Seoul, Korea, looking like a total emotional wreck. I knocked on his door. That old Nazarene missionary, Merrill Williams, opened the door and just stared deeply into my eyes for a while. Then he spoke. "You look like an emotional train wreck." Old friends have a way with words, don't they!

Merrill took me to Taechon Beach on the west coast of Korea, where years ago our families vacationed together every August. It was Easter weekend. Somewhere along my desperate path, I had picked up a book about the seven last sayings of Christ on the cross. I began to read the seven chapters and slowly share with Merrill my personal perspective on my miserable existence. Merrill patiently listened. I read eagerly about the feeling Jesus had when he said from the cross, "My God, My God, Why?" Exactly! That's where I was. I didn't have a clue why God had allowed all of these things to happen to me and my family. We were diligently serving Him, yet it all blew up in our faces.

Jesus' words continued. "God, why have you forsaken me?" For His utter honesty and for the way He questioned God's goodness, Jesus suddenly became my long lost hero. "That's right, Jesus! You tell God off! Let it all out! He needs to hear it! I'm right behind you doing the same!" All I could pray was, "God, I feel like you have abandoned me just when

I needed You most. Why has all this happened? Why have You forsaken me? Why?"

Even though I had a good friend to talk to, I left Merrill in his beach cabin by himself and went out on a rocky point over the ocean. I felt like I was going to explode inside. Sitting down on a large rock, I opened up the book to read about the next saying of Christ on the cross. I was hoping for more opportunity to vent my anger to God, but what I found in the next saying of Christ from the cross served as a life changing reality check for poor old me.

"Into your hands I commit my spirit."

What? My hero said *that?* What's going on here? Suddenly the truth hit me straight in the heart. *My misery was due to my focus on self.* I had insisted on having *my* way–being in *my* place, living in *my* home, being with *my* family, doing *my* work; *my, my, my.* After all, I was a missionary, and that gave me an automatic halo!

Because there had been so much spiritual fruit from sharing the gospel, I had assumed that my heart was in the right place. I had even been training other people in how to do evangelism that resulted in new, simple churches. I had been telling people, "I want to help you take your work to the next level." In my pride, little did I know that what needed to go the next level was my heart! I had forced God to go to great lengths to show me the true condition of my heart. I was a believer, and though I had given my life to the Lordship of Jesus Christ, I had taken the control of my life back into my own hands. When the reality of my heart condition suddenly became clear, in an instant my anger against God turned to embarrassment before His face.

I was so tired from the emotional turmoil within. In that moment I bowed my knees down onto the uncomfortably hard rock underneath me and prayed to God. "I give up. I'm through. I just will think of myself as dead now. I give You my spirit. Replace my spirit with Your Spirit. I surrender. You win. I'm finished. I finally get it." My voice had the tone of someone who had struggled against an enemy for a long time and had finally come before the enemy to surrender. I had been reduced to total dependence on God.

Then I got up off my knees and stood up straight, looking out across the ocean as if I were seeing it for the first time. The ocean reminded me of the greatness of God. He was in control, and I had tried to be the one controlling my life. Slowly, I began to sing, "All to Jesus I surrender. All to Him I freely give. I will ever love and trust Him, in His presence daily live. I surrender all. I surrender all. All to Thee my blessed Savior, I surrender all."

Something changed deep within me that day. Almost like being literally lifted off the earth, I felt myself die. I saw life, not from my own perspective, but from God's eyes. Gone from me was the question, "Why?" I don't need to know why. I know "Who." He is enough. Gone is the restlessness. It's His life, not mine. It's His work, not mine.

It's possible, my friend, that you are doing all the right things and yet you do not have a right heart before God. That's a restless place to be. If there is one thing that you take away from our time together in these pages, take away God as the center of who you are and why you are. Circumstances will sometimes disappoint. Life is not always fair. Sometimes people are unpredictable. However, God will never disappoint the one whose heart is stayed on Him.

Consider this lifestyle: putting God at the very center of who you are and why you are. What are the advantages of such a life? When a person has God as the true reason for living, when God is free to direct the person's thoughts and actions, then that person has a whole heart. That person is doing the right thing consistently, and for the right motive. Proverbs describes such a person as "righteous," and continually promises that God blesses a righteous person.

Blessings are on the head of the righteous.
Proverbs 10:6 (NIV)

A righteous person is able to find the right course of action each day in life because the person has truly surrendered self to the Lordship of Creator God. Being righteous does not mean simply doing what you think is right.

Every man's way is right in his own eyes,
but the Lord weighs the hearts.
Proverbs 21:2 (NIV)

Being a righteous person is first a matter of the heart. Simply trying to do the right thing will not cause a person to be righteous. Man cannot do the right thing without surrendering the will to the Creator. Remember? The human condition is one of delusion–thinking, "I'm in control here."

All the ways of a man are clean in his own sight, but the Lord weighs the motives. Proverbs 16:2 (NASV)

Living right begins with the heart, not the hands. Our bodies can be making all the right motions, but if our hearts are far from God, He sees the motive behind the movement and is not pleased. We can go into a church building, stand when we are supposed to stand, open the Bible when we are supposed to, and close our eyes when we are supposed to pray. However, that doesn't make us right with God any more than going into McDonalds makes us a Big Mac. We can deceive ourselves and others, but we can't fake God out.

When it comes to righteousness, there is another form of self-deception. If we think that righteousness is *only* a matter of the heart, we are in error. We tell ourselves, when doing wrong, that, "What I'm doing now is alright because I have a good heart, and God sees my heart." Righteousness begins in the heart, but it must not stop there. Righteousness means *doing* the right thing from a good heart. God sees what we do as well as the motive of the heart.

For the ways of a man are before the eyes of the Lord, and He watches all his paths."
Proverbs 5:21 (NASV) See also 15:3

When a person has a right relationship with God from the heart, and the hands are in sync with the heart, life is as it was meant to be. There is integrity. The person is whole. All parts of life are flowing correctly together into the simple, solo life core of God Himself. Only by realizing God is in control and surrendering to His control do we find that life begins to work *for* us instead of against us. You can experience the tremendous peace and power of a truly integrated, righteous life. How insecure man feels when he puts life into his own hands! How big the hands of God, and how secure the person who places his life in those hands.

For the Lord will be your confidence, and will keep your foot from being caught. Proverbs 3:26 (NASV)

God heaps promise after promise on to those who will pursue righteousness. It's enough to make you wonder why anyone would be crazy enough *not* to sign up to be on God's team!

- "For the Lord...stores up *wisdom* for the upright.
- He is *a shield* to those who walk in integrity, *guarding the paths* of justice, and He *preserves* the way of His godly ones" (Proverbs 2:6–8, NASV, emphasis mine).
- "He *is intimate* with the upright...He *blesses the dwelling* of the righteous" (Proverbs 3:32–33, NASV, emphasis mine).
- "The way of the Lord is a *stronghold* to the upright... The righteous will *never be shaken*" (Proverbs 10:29–30, NASV, emphasis mine).
- "The prayer of the upright is *His delight*...He *loves* him who pursues righteousness" (Proverbs 15:9, NASV, emphasis mine).
- "When a man's ways are pleasing to the Lord, He makes even his enemies to be at peace with him" (Proverbs 16:7, NASV, emphasis mine).
- "The name of the Lord is a *strong tower*. The righteous runs into it, and is *safe*" (Proverbs 18:10, NASV, emphasis mine).
- "In the way of righteousness is *life*" (Proverbs 12:28, NASV, emphasis mine).

Wow! What a good deal. We get into a tough spot in life and realize we need God, so we make a deal with Him. "God, I promise to be good if you fix this mess I made." Then, however, when everything starts going well again, we forget God and resume the "I'm in control" delusion once again. Has that ever happened to you? How do we *maintain* a right heart and right habits? It is impossible outside a right relationship with God. Proverbs gives us six commands for keeping a right relationship with God. What are those six commands? We are to *fear* the Lord, *trust* in the Lord, *acknowledge* Him in all our ways, *honor* Him with our wealth, *accept* the Lord's discipline, and *commit* our works to Him. Let's take these one at a time.

Fear the Lord

Do not be wise in your own eyes.
Fear the Lord and turn away from evil.
Proverbs 3:7 (NASV)

The fear of the Lord is the beginning of knowledge.
Proverbs 1:7 (NASV)
The fear of the Lord is the beginning of wisdom,
and the knowledge of the Holy One is understanding.
Proverbs 9:10 (NASV)

We tend to think of fear as a negative thing. What benefits could possibly come from something as politically incorrect as fear? Is there anything to gain from fearing God? There are so many benefits.

- "The fear of the Lord *prolongs life*" (Proverbs 10:27, NASV, emphasis mine).
- "The fear of the Lord is the beginning of *wisdom*" (Proverbs 9:10, NASV, emphasis mine).
- "Fear the Lord and turn away from evil. It will be *healing* to your body, and *refreshment* to your bones" (Proverbs 3:7–8, NASV, emphasis mine).
- "In the fear of the Lord there is strong *confidence,* and His children will have *refuge.* The fear of the Lord is a fountain of *life,* that one may avoid the snares of death" (Proverbs 14:26–27, NASV, emphasis mine). (See also Proverbs 16:6)
- "The reward of humility and the fear of the Lord are *riches, honor,* and *life*" (Proverbs 22:4, NASV, emphasis mine).

How does a person go about fearing God? Are we to have a sense of dread? Are we to coil into a corner at the thought of Him? Notice three things you must do to consistently fear God.

- First, you must not be impressed with yourself. "Do not be wise in your own eyes" (Proverbs 3:7, NASV). Don't think of yourself as having all the answers. Don't turn to your own intellect before you turn to God. Fearing God means you realize He not only *has* the answers, He *is* The Answer. Do you realize your own limited ability to think straight?
- Second, you must "turn away from evil" (Proverbs 3:7, NASV). You must love Holy God so much that you are sickened by sin. Fearing God means you love purity and hate evil. "The fear of the Lord is

to hate evil" (Proverbs 8:13 NASV). Is there moral compromise in your life right now?

- Third, you must "make your ear attentive to wisdom...then you will discern the fear of the Lord, and discover the knowledge of God" (Proverbs 2:2, 5). Fearing God means that you are desperate to know and please Him; you continually seek to discover His wisdom for your life. Is your ear tuned more to your own voice than to God's voice?

Though it is not always easy to describe what it means to fear the Lord, it is easy to see when someone has no fear of God: the self-reliance, the pride, the haughtiness, and the daredevil approach to life that defies authority of any kind. Life's motto is "No Fear." This person's heart becomes hard, and he or she refuses to fear God. Though God is patient, such a lifestyle of defiance does not go unnoticed by God. If you do not fear God, God says that you may eventually hit rock bottom and see your need for the Lord, "when your dread comes like a storm, and your calamity comes on like a whirlwind, when distress and anguish come on you" (Proverbs 1:27, NASV). What is God's response then? "They will call on me, but I will not answer; they will seek me diligently but they shall not find me, because they hated knowledge, and did not choose the fear of the Lord" (Proverbs 1:28–30, NASV). This is a clear warning given to those who do not fear God. Fear the Lord while there is still time.

Trust in the Lord

Trust in the Lord with all your heart,
and do not lean on your own understanding.
Proverbs 3:5 (NASV)

The word "trust" is used to describe a baby resting peacefully in mother's arms (Psalms 22:9). Trust is pictured also as lying helplessly face down (Jeremiah 12:5). This face down position in Old Testament times signified one of two possibilities. A servant lay face down to the ground whenever he came before the master. The position showed the total surrender of self to master. The servant lying face down on the ground before the master was completely ready to obey. The other time someone would assume such a position was a soldier when he was defeated. The captured soldier would lie face down before his new general. He yielded himself unconditionally to the conquering general.

Have you been conquered by Christ the King? Who is your commanding officer? Do you give Him a brief nod of the head occasionally as you strut proudly through life, or do you lie helplessly face down on the ground before Him? Is this issue of who's in charge of your life still leaving you restless inside? Come as a child into the Father's arms and find peace there.

Have you given up yet? Surrender. I was confronted by the Commander General that day on the shore of Korea. He commanded that He conquer me in totality. I could have ignored His command, and continued in my misery. But I chose to fall face down and yield myself to Him like I never had before. Am I ever glad I did! What power comes into the life of one who has abandoned all self-direction! He commands this of you: fall face down before your conquering General. Trust into His care and direction all your heart, your mind, your relationships, your finances, your emotions, your everything. Forget about diversifying the investment of self. Bet your whole life on God. He will not disappoint.

Do not lean on your own understanding.
Proverbs 3:5 (NASV)

The word "lean" is the idea of supporting yourself–putting your physical weight onto something that you hope will hold you up. Lean your life's weight onto the flimsy stick of your own intellect and sense of direction, and that stick will snap out from underneath you! You weigh too much! And that stick never was designed to hold your weight!

Here you are on the shore of life's ocean. You've seen the distant island of the blessed life. It *is* out there. And you know it. You assumed the way to get there was by learning how to swim. So everyday you've been putting the flippers on and venturing out a little farther into the ocean. The current is so strong you've never made it out to that beautiful place of paradise—not yet anyway. Suddenly one day as you are training yourself for the good life, a blue boat pulls up. That's never happened before. This is a swimming beach, not a boat dock. You notice the boat has no motors, not even inboard ones. And no sails. The Captain says, "Wanna go to the island, don't you?"

"How did you know that?"

The Captain just chuckles softly and says, "These things

were determined way back when I wrote eternity on your heart."

"What was that you said? You wrote eternity in my heart?"

"I'll explain it later. For now, just get in. There's no other way to get there."

Hesitantly, you respond, "Why should I trust you? Your boat doesn't even have a motor or anything."

"Wanna get to the island, don't you? I will get you there."

You push away from the shoreline of your own swimming ability, and leaving your ambition behind, climb into the boat of the Captain's love and power. Both exhausted from your prior struggles and relieved to surrender self to the Captain of Eternity, you fall face down in the bottom of the boat. The Captain wills the boat to go forward through His own power, and it takes off. Though the sea is rough and the boat ride is choppy, inside the boat you feel like a child back in the security of Mother's womb.

Blessed is he who trusts in the Lord.
Proverbs 16:20 (NASV)

Then the Captain walks over, lifts up your head, looks approvingly into your eyes, and says warmly, "Welcome aboard. Come stand by me at the wheel." Stand by the Captain at the wheel? Wow! What an honor!

He who trusts in the Lord will be exalted.
Proverbs 29:25 (NASV)

Later, you ask the Captain, "What was that You said about eternity in my heart?"

He replies,

Man's steps are ordained by the Lord,
How then can man understand his way?
Proverbs 20:24 (NASV)

You realize then that as a mere man, you cannot lean on your own understanding. You've known all along that you've never really understood how to find your own way through life. However, the Captain had a specific purpose for your life before you were even born. The Paradise Island you've longed for is arrived at by finding God's will for your life. Trust Him to bring His ordained plan to fruition. Fully submit yourself to the Captain.

Acknowledge Him in All Your Ways

In all your ways acknowledge Him, and He will make your paths straight. Proverbs 3:6 (NASV)

Here we have a key secret of how to find the right course of action every time. The word "acknowledge" literally means to "know." Know God intimately in each situation, and He will make it clear what you are to do. Until He makes it clear, you must continue to know Him more intimately. Recognize Him before every turn in life, even in the small things and even in the things that seem obvious.

By the time I was nineteen, I had already enjoyed four

years of recognition as a radio disc jockey. I worked at a large popular music station. KROK in Shreveport, Louisiana was the station that everybody listened to for rock music. And I was their weekend star! After my first year of university, they offered me a full time slot, doing mid-days from ten to two. Four hours of work every day for full time pay; that was a no-brainer. I began looking forward to the last day of school when I would begin full time work.

Then strange things started to happen. My path was no longer straight. I became confused. Why was food no longer tasty? Why was I finding it difficult to go to sleep at night? Why were my friends saying I was no fun anymore? Then I knew. I remembered that I had applied to go as a summer missionary to who knows where for ten weeks, doing who knows what, for next to nothing in pay. I began to realize I had done what was right in my own eyes, without consulting God. The decision to work as a full time DJ seemed so obvious at the time. However, I was leaning on that old cracked stick of my own understanding, and it had broken under my weight. As soon as I began to pray, I knew what to do. My path became straight once again.

I went to Washington and Idaho that summer and had such a great time serving the Lord that I asked Him for the privilege of serving Him full time for the rest of my life. To this day, He has granted my request. As fervently and as consistently as possible, I want to know and do His will. That's the sweet spot in this life. I want to live "in the zone." By acknowledging God in the decision of how I would spend my summer, the entire direction of my life changed, as did my immediate future. Within a short period of time, the great radio station KROK went bankrupt and went off the air. Had I leaned on my own understanding, I would have gone down with the radio station.

The world of animal behavior has discovered that baby animals who cannot find their mother can become attached to a female animal of a different species. The baby treats her as mother. For instance, a baby rabbit could not find his mother, but found instead a stray female cat. The cat began allowing the rabbit to drink her milk. The rabbit began imitating the lifestyle of the cat. This phenomenon is known as "bonding." We are to become personally bonded to the Lord. We look to Him for everything we need in life. We see Him with a combined sense of awe, intimacy, and obligation. We are utterly dependent on Him. We seek to be like Him. If you are not there yet, I invite you to pray a bold request to the Lord:

"God, reduce me to total dependence on You."

When we live in continual awareness of the Lord, we have a deep sense of well being. Self is whole, thriving, and radiant. Total, personal well being is God's gift to those who walk closely with Him. The whole person is invigorated. Gone is the feeling of floundering through life. He makes your paths straight.

He is a shield to those who take refuge in Him.
Proverbs 30:5 (NASV)

Seek to know the Father in all areas of your life. Make Him more than your co-pilot. Let Him completely direct your way. Is He Lord of your relationships? Is He in charge of your attitudes? Is He happy with the words you say? Do you consult Him in the little decisions of your life, even the seemingly obvious ones? Is He pleased with where you go?

Is your heart right before Him? Does He have control of your pocket book?

Honor the Lord with Your Wealth

Honor the Lord with your wealth,
And from the first of all your produce;
So your barns will be filled with plenty,
And your vats will over flow with new wine.
Proverbs 3:9-10 (NASV)

In a church, in the deep South of the United States, the preacher was moving toward the end of his sermon, and with a growing crescendo he said, "This church, like the crippled man, has got to get up and walk."

And the congregation responded, "That's right, preacher. Let it walk."

And he added, "This church, like Elijah on Mount Carmel, has got to run."

"Run, let it run, preacher. Let it run."

"This church has got to mount up on wings like eagles and fly."

"Let it fly, preacher. Let it fly."

Then he added, "Now if this church is going to fly, it's gonna take money!"

"Let it walk, preacher. Let it walk."

We all tend to hold on tightly to our money. We work hard to fill our own barns. Of course, if our barns ever do get filled, we do have the thought of maybe giving God some of the overflow–later. Then, however, once the money is in hand, we start thinking about how we need a bigger barn so we can store up even more. We have it all backwards.

God says honor Him by giving to Him right off the top. Make it the first thing you do when you are paid. The people of the Old Testament gave the first of every ten animals and the first of every ten fruits of the vine and all produce to the Lord. They were constantly reminded that the flocks and fields belonged to God. In the face of our desire to keep, giving is a simple test of our faith that God will provide our needs. Giving our first and our best to God is a way of recognizing that we are stewards. All that we have belongs to God.

God promises this:

The Lord will not allow the righteous to hunger.
Proverbs 10:3 (NASV)

Test Him. Give to Him as soon as you get paid every month. Give at least the amount shown in the Bible as a giving pattern: ten percent of gross income. See if God does not give you all that you need and bless you in other ways as well. Your barns are not best filled by you. Give to God first and let Him fill your barns. He will supply all your needs as you honor Him with your wealth.

One young rich man responded to such a challenge by saying that he could not possibly give ten percent. It was just way too much money. An elderly believer came to the young man and said, “I’ll pray for you, then. I’ll pray that God will reduce your income down to the point where you’ll be able to give as you should.” The rich man fell under the Lord’s discipline.

Accept the Lord's Discipline

My son, do not reject the discipline of the Lord, or loathe His reproof, for who the Lord loves He reproves, even as a father, the son in whom he delights.
Proverbs 3:11-12 (NASV)

A good father points out a child's willful defiance. He does so in love, helping the child to become teachable. Children enter the world with a bent toward selfishness and a tendency to refuse discipline. When I was a boy, we lived in a house that had a storage room off the carport. My bicycle was in that storage room. I rode my bike almost daily, so it was my responsibility to keep that storage room locked. One day I forgot to lock the storage room. My Father asked me if I had locked it. I knew I had not, and he knew I had not, but I said that I had. My parents were grieved at my refusal to take ownership for my actions. Days later I finally admitted that I had not locked the room. My father made the storage room an issue because he wanted me to grow up to be responsible and to admit my mistakes. He cared enough about me to train me in doing what's right. Successful adults generally look back to firm, loving parents who took the initiative to discipline them in the early years.

Why are we prone to hide our own mistakes? Why do we shrink from being disciplined? Discipline pinches our pride. One reason God disciplines us is to remove pride from our hearts.

The Lord will tear down the house of the proud.
Proverbs 15:25 (NASV)

Pride tells us to say that we locked the door when we really didn't. Pride tells us to cover up our own faults. We want to appear better than we are, but we cannot deceive God. Then if we work to deceive others, making them think we are someone we really aren't, we grow weary of faking it. Eventually, we will be found out and our house of cards will tumble down.

The refining pot is for silver and the furnace for gold,
but the Lord tests the hearts.
Proverbs 17:3 (NASV)

Another reason why God disciplines us is to purify our character. Gold is refined by very hot fire. When the heat is on, the impurities within the gold rise to the top. The refiner then scrapes away those impurities. What's left is solid gold. The craftsman is then free to form the pure metal into an object of beauty and usefulness. Without the fire, the gold is impure and unfit for use. Only through the Refiner's fire do we become purged of our impurities. Submit your heart to His fire today. He will make you pure, beautiful, and useful.

How does God break through into our lives and correct us? How do we feel the Refiner's fire on our lives? Does lightning fall from heaven? Do we receive God's new directions for us by accidentally slipping on a banana peel and landing on a map giving us our new GPS coordinates? Sometimes God does use very drastic means to get our attention, but usually He speaks through small voices more than thunder. God disciplines us through His word (Proverbs 30:5–6), through friends and mentors (Proverbs 27:6, 9, 17; 28:23), through situations (Proverbs 15:5), and through the conscience He placed within us. "The spirit of man is the lamp of the Lord, searching all the innermost parts of his being" (Proverbs 20:27, NASV). Which of these is God using in your life lately to re-direct your path? He is seeking to change your heart. How are you responding to His correction? Pray "Change my heart oh God. Let me be like You."

He who neglects discipline despises himself,
but he who listens to reproof acquires understanding.
Proverbs 15:32 (NASV)

When we ignore criticism, we only hurt ourselves. How do you respond when God corrects you? "Poverty and shame will come to him who neglects discipline, but he who regards reproof will be honored" (Proverbs 13:18, NASV). To live by instinct alone, never changing your actions and attitudes, is to reduce yourself to live as a mere animal. However, if you become a life-long learner, each day is an opportunity to be refined by fire. Each person is someone from whom you can learn. Each situation is an opportunity for God to mold you into new form. The challenge for you and me is clear: willingly and thankfully accept criticism and correction as a gift. Being disciplined is an opportunity to learn, grow, and change.

Let's practice what that would look like. Father says

to his son, "Matthew, you forgot to lock the storage room, didn't you?"

Matthew suddenly feels an urge to cover for himself and save himself the trouble of going out to lock the door. Then he realizes his Father is just trying to help him develop a good habit, and keep his bike from getting stolen. So instead he says, "Yes, you are right. I didn't lock it. I'll go do it now. Thank you." Dad is shocked by his young son's maturity and blesses him with a big grin and hug.

You can't whitewash your sins and get by with it;
you find mercy by admitting and leaving them.
Proverbs 28:13 (The Message)

When disciplined, confess you are in the wrong. When God points out an area of needed change in your life, thank Him and agree with Him. Then enjoy His love–a love that will not leave you alone to follow your own error. These days, are you feeling the Refiner's fire? Let Him burn away your impurities, leaving you beautiful, useful, and pure as gold. Respond to discipline with humble change, and you are gold in the making!

Commit Your Works to the Lord

Commit your works to the Lord,
and your plans will be established.
Proverbs 16:3 (NASV)

The word "commit "means "to roll over onto." When

you place over onto God all your efforts, then your plans can become solid reality. Rolling over your plans onto Him means exchanging a self-directed life for a God directed life. I dare you to live the exchanged life. Lay down the arrogance of self-made plans and the pride of self-directed living. Take on the habit of humbly placing onto God your daily work and your planning procedure.

Some think that believers should not plan. Their motto is, "let go and let God." Nowhere in scripture do we find those words. God blesses the diligent, wise planner. Failure to plan is a sure sign of laziness. God wants us to strategize. He wants us to dream big. Nothing is impossible. He wants to sit at the CEO chair during our strategy meetings. He wants to be the chief strategist, and He wants us to become His field agent. To plan without God at the center of it is arrogance. To plan with God's glory as the goal brings great focus, purpose, and joy to the work and the worker.

God expects us to prayerfully make plans. He wants us to submit those plans to Him and let Him make the final decision. When we make our plans His, they become no less ours. We are still responsible and accountable before God for the work. Put God in charge of your work. Then what you've planned will take place as He shows you how to do it.

The horse is prepared for the day of battle,
but victory belongs to the Lord.
Proverbs 21:31 (NASV)

We are to saddle up our horses. Get ready for the grand adventure and spiritual battle of following the Lord. Remember, He is the General marching before us. Move out at His command. Don't run ahead on your own. Don't sit on your rear on the back row either. Be on the front line, mounted on your horse, ready to move at the sound of His voice. The battle belongs to the Lord.

The mind of man plans his way,
but the Lord directs his steps.
Proverbs 16:9 (NASV)

Are you a novice, wanting to become a competent expert? We've all seen in the movies the business executive who has huge decisions to make, involving millions of dollars and the employment of hundreds of people. For you and me, making such decisions would be seriously stressful. However, the executive simply gathers a few facts, has a few discussions, and makes the right decisions in a short time. Maybe you play chess. Toward the end of the game, you find it hard to make the right moves. It may take you five or ten minutes to consider all the options before you choose one. Then one day as you surf the cable channels, you notice a professional chess tournament where experts are making moves in less than six seconds! How can they do that?

How can we make decisions like an expert? Books have been written attempting to teach people how to think like such competent decision makers. Yet the key to making the right decision every time is *not* in learning to *think* like an expert. It's in learning to *learn* like an expert. What makes an expert an expert? He or she is doing three things.

1. The expert is learning from other experts.
2. He or she is a life-long learner.

3. The expert is piling up wisdom gleamed from experiences.

The novice systematically gathers facts and scientifically compares options. The expert relies on intuition and perceptiveness to quickly see what to him is obviously the best move.[41] As The Expert, God wants to be our teacher. Life itself is the classroom. But there is tuition to pay, and it's pricey. You see, in order to enroll, we must roll over everything onto God, exchanging self-help for Divine direction.

In his old book, *Victorious Christian Living,* Alan Redpath gives us an example of the exchanged life. Home in England for new recruits after years on the mission field, Hudson Taylor sat in contemplation one day and became conscious as never before of his helplessness and unworthiness and uselessness in the service of God. Then, to quote his own words, he recognized that "it is not what Hudson Taylor does for God that matters, but what God does through Hudson Taylor." And from that day he commenced to live what he called the "exchanged life," in which it was "no more I, but Christ."[42]

Don't compartmentalize your life, making your faith just one component. God must become more to you than someone with Whom you make deals, worship on Sunday, and pray to before meals. He must become the One for whom you live. Make the Father CEO of your daily life.

We have looked at the six commands that Proverbs gives to help us have a right relationship with God. We are to fear the Lord, trust Him, acknowledge Him in all our ways, honor Him with our wealth, accept His discipline, and commit our works to Him. Following these commands helps us to do the right things consistently, to choose the right way every time.

But do not be deceived. We cannot live righteously on our own. There is not one single righteous person, except for Jesus Christ. Proverbs points to the Savior. When we put our trust in Him, then we find the recipe for living wisely. Jesus speaks in Proverbs, saying,

> From everlasting I was established, from the beginning, from the earliest times of the earth...Before the mountains were settled, before the hills I was brought forth...When He established the heavens, I was there, when He inscribed a circle on the face of the deep, when He made firm the skies above, when the springs of the deep became fixed, when He set for the sea its boundary, so that the water should not transgress His command, when He marked out the foundations of the earth; Then I was beside Him, as a master workman; and I was His delight...Now therefore, o sons, listen to me, For blessed are they who keep my ways...For he who finds Me finds life (Proverbs 8:23–30, 32, 35, NASV).

And now someone greater than Solomon is here.
Matthew 12:42

EPILOGUE

We've spent an entire book learning the wisdom of Solomon. There are still more timeless truths from Proverbs which I hope to share with you in the future. Solomon was a good wisdom coach. *However, he was not the best.* Now at the end, we realize that someone greater than Solomon is here. Solomon compiled wisdom and *taught* wisdom but didn't always *live* wisdom. Jesus *is* wisdom, personified. He wants to change your life.

What do you need to do for lasting change to occur in your life?

- Tell the creator God that you sincerely regret not having lived with Him as your center. Admit to Him that you have been self-centered. Tell Him you want to turn your life over to Him and start over.

- Ask God to forgive you. Thank Him for coming to this earth as Jesus and showing you the way. Praise Him for loving you enough to die for you on the cross. Tell Him that through Jesus' resurrection, you want to be made into a new person. Let the Holy Spirit fill your being.
- Get involved in a local church where transparent relationships are happening through Bible teaching, worship, and small groups. Share this decision you have made with people there. They will baptize you, and help you follow Jesus.
- Share the joy and purpose you find in Jesus with others regularly.

Life is about changing into who God wants you to be. Are you serious about following God's recipe for living wisely? Then get ready for a grand adventure! You are in for the time of your life! Open your life and pour in Proverbs!

TO CONTACT THE AUTHOR

Matthew and Cheryl Nance often lead seminars on a variety of topics related to Christian living. They are certified by Ken Blanchard to facilitate "Lead like Jesus," a two to four day highly relational seminar designed to help people become more effective as leaders. They also frequently lead interactive seminars on "Raising Boys," "Setting Boundaries," "Strategic Missions Thinking," and more. The Nances lead Marriage Enrichment seminars and interactive sessions coaching missionaries in work related issues. Matthew enjoys preaching, and has spoken in over 150 churches in the U.S. and internationally.

To contact Matthew about a speaking engagement, write nancefamily@mail.com To help him write more effectively in the future, Matthew would like to receive your response to *Living Wisely*.

ENDNOTES

1 Bruce Marchiano, *In The Footsteps of Jesus* (Eugene, Oregon, Harvest House Publishers, 1996), 154.
2 Clyde Murdock, *A Treasury of Humor,* as quoted in Charles R. Swindoll, *Swindoll's Ultimate Book of Illustrations & Quotes* (Nashville, Thomas Nelson, 1998), 33.
3 Charles R. Swindoll, *Hope Again,* as quoted in Charles R. Swindoll, *Swindoll's Ultimate Book of Illustrations & Quotes,* 493.
4 See Genesis 1:28–31
5 Harvey Mackay, *We Got Fired...And It's the Best Thing That Ever Happened to Us* (New York, Ballantine Books, 2004), 252.
6 See S. Truett Cathy, *Eat Mor Chikin, Inspire More People: Doing Business the Chick-fil-a Way* (Decatur, Looking Glass Books, 2002).
7 Ken Blanchard and Phil Hodges, *Lead Like Jesus* (Nashville, W Publishing Group, 2005), 53.
8 Harvey Mackay, *We Got Fired,* 225.
9 Merrill Oster and Mike Hamel, *The Entrepreneur's Creed* (Singapore, Armour 2003), 101.
10 See Psalm 141:3, James 3:10, and Ephesians 4:29.
11 Sam Levenson, *You Don't Have to Be in Who's Who to Know What's What* (Simon & Schuster, 1980).
12 See Ken Blanchard and Phil Hodge's website www.leadlikejesus.com.
13 You may also speak life to others by quoting verses like Exodus 19:5, Psalm 71:6, Psalm 139:16, Jeremiah 1:4–5, and Ephesians 1:4.
14 For more on this subject, see John C. Maxwell, *Winning with People* (Nashville, Tn. 2004).
15 See the "Healing Words" website at www.uab.edu/healingwords/index.php.

16 See Proverbs 27:14 for a case of very bad verbal timing!

17 Lee Strobel, *The Case for Faith* (Grand Rapids, Mich Zondervan, 2000), 101.

18 Robert Jeffress, *The Solomon Secrets* (Colorado Springs, Co.: Waterbrook Press, 2002), 206.

19 Jeffress, 209.

20 Charles R. Swindoll, *The Quest for Character* (Zondervan, 1993).

21 See I Kings 3:1.

22 See I Kings 4:1–25.

23 *International Standard Bible Encyclopedia* (Grand Rapids: Eerdmans 1984), 2822–2825.

24 See I Kings 4:29–34.

25 Phillip Caputo, "Alone," included in *Wild Stories: The Best of Men's Journal* (New York: Three Rivers Press, 2002) 91.

26 Dinah Maria Mulock Craik, *A Life for a Life* (London: Collins' Clear Type Press 1900), Chapter XVI.

27 Erwin Raphael McManus, *Uprising: A Revolution of the Soul* (Thomas Nelson, 2003), 148.

28 "Lean on Me," by Bill Withers.

29 Though Drew's heart was in the right place, Drew and others need to realize that doing acts of service is for the sake of man as well as for the sake of God.

30 Gary Inrig, *Quality of Friendship.*

31 http://thinkexist.com/quotes/jay_kesler/, as quoted from Jay Kesler, *Being Holy Being Human* (Bethany House 1994).

32 Bill Hybels and Rob Wilkins, *Find True Satisfaction by Descending Into Greatness* (Grand Rapids, Zondervan 1993), 130.

33 Ibid, 137.

34 Adapted from Dr. Henry Cloud and Dr. John Townsend, *Making Dating Work: Boundaries in Dating* (Grand Rapids, Zondervan 2000), 173.

35 Richard Exley, *How to be a Man of Character in a World of Compromise; Insights from the Book of Proverbs* (Tulsa, Honor Books, 1995), 35.

36 Stu Weber, *Spirit Warriors* (Sisters, Oregon, Multnomah Publishers, 2001), 200.

37 *International Standard Bible Encyclopedia*, 2825b.

38 Charles R. Swindoll, *Come Before Winter and Share My Hope* (Carol Stream, Illinois, Tyndale, 1988).

39 Spiros Zodhiates, *The Behavior of Belief (*Grand Rapids, Michigan: Eerdmans Publishing Company, 1970).

40 For vivid examples of this in Bangladesh, and perhaps the best case study of a sustained effort in lifting people out of poverty, see Muhammad Yunus, *Creating a World Without Poverty* (New York, Public Affairs, 2007).

41 For more on this, see Gary Klein, *Sources of Power: How People Make Decisions* (London, MIT Press, 1999).

42 Alan Redpath, *Victorious Christian Living* (London: Fleming H. Revell, MCMLV -1955), 251.

OTHER BOOKS FROM THE AUTHOR

Printed in the United States
By Bookmasters